Jai Yen Means Keep A Cool Heart

Life Among The Mountain Tribes Of Thailand

RUPERT NELSON

Bloomington, IN  Milton Keynes, UK

authorHOUSE®

AuthorHouse™
1663 Liberty Drive, Suite 200
Bloomington, IN 47403
www.authorhouse.com
Phone: 1-800-839-8640

AuthorHouse™ UK Ltd.
500 Avebury Boulevard
Central Milton Keynes, MK9 2BE
www.authorhouse.co.uk
Phone: 08001974150

First published by AuthorHouse 9/26/2006

ISBN: 1-4259-4580-5 (sc)

Library of Congress Control Number: 2006905649

Printed in the United States of America
Bloomington, Indiana

This book is printed on acid-free paper.

This book is dedicated to the three women in my life, to whom I have tried to be a good husband and a good father.

Dee, Rebecca and Lani

PREFACE

When my wife, Dee, and I first applied for overseas mission work we were turned down. Big, big disappointment.

As a soldier during the Korean War I saw many starving and freezing children. The experience tore at my heart and gave me a desire to help those locked in such poverty. To that end, after the war, I got a Masters Degree in Agriculture, while Dee, also interested in mission work, became a high school Home Economics teacher. But our dreams, apparently, were not to be.

I found employment with the Montana Agricultural Extension Service on the Fort Peck Indian Reservation and for more than three years we lived and worked with the Lakota and Assiniboine Native Americans. I learned how to live and work in a cross-cultural situation with customs and traditions quite foreign to me, a South Dakota farm boy. Many of my lessons were of the type not found in books.

Then, suddenly, the door to Thailand opened. Not simply Thailand: the Mountain Tribes in northern Thailand had requested the American Baptist Mission to send an Agricultural Advisor to work with them to improve their livelihood. It seemed the perfect fit for my skills. What I didn't realize at the time was the uncanny similarities the mountain people of Thailand had with my Native American friends. Without knowing it, our three years in Montana had prepared us for this very mission.

It was the first of many "interesting" events I have experienced first-hand during our 33 years of work in Thailand. I thought of my grandfather, the Rev. Peter Clemens Larsen, and one of his favorite expressions. When events worked out miraculously well he would exclaim, "My, my, wasn't that providential?" Knowing him, he would want that word spelled with a capitol "P".

Thailand changed me in many ways. I learned to be *jai yen*, which means to keep a cool heart and not get too excited or angry, but keep a cool exterior. That is the Thai way.

This book is a collection of stories and events that happened to me and my family while adjusting to a different culture and roaming the hills of Northern Thailand.

Providential? I'll let you, the reader, be the judge of that.

Table of Contents

THE ARRIVAL

I sat staring out the window at the view below as our Thai Airways plane began its descent to Don Muang Airport near Bangkok. The flat, flooded rice paddies extended from horizon to horizon. Small villages, bordered by an occasional canal, offered the only relief in the emerald green brightness reflecting the late afternoon sun. My wife, Dee, and three year old daughter, Lani, sat in the seats next to me. We were expecting our second child in about four months. Lani was sound asleep, oblivious to the changes about to take place in her life. I was very much aware of those changes. The funny feeling in the pit of my stomach that day was not caused by air travel. What kind of experiences would we have in this land, the Kingdom of Thailand, where we had volunteered to live and work? We knew so little about Thailand, or Siam as it was formerly called, and yet we intended to live there for many years. On that day we were perched on the edge of a divide between the familiar old and the unknown new.

Some would have thought us a strangely put together family; a product of the new world that formed after World War II. Dee of Chinese heritage from Hawaii, me a Midwest farm boy of Danish extraction, and Lani, a Lakota Sioux, whom we had adopted at the age of 10 months. Dee and I were looking

1

forward to living and working in a different culture, but we felt some trepidation as well. We really didn't know what to expect. Were we foolish to leave family, friends and the familiar places of our homeland?

It was evening when we disembarked at Don Muang International Airport that warm October day in 1963. It felt as if we had walked into a hot, sticky oven. Within minutes we were perspiring heavily and our American clothing stuck to our bodies. It was not like the cool crispness of Montana evenings.

"Hello Nelsons! Welcome to Thailand." Cheery voices hailed us from the top of the air terminal building. The voices turned out to belong to the Carders and Gregories, who served with the Mission in Bangkok. They drove us to the Bangkok Christian Guest House, where we were to stay for a few days. We started learning about Thailand during the trip in from the airport. First, we noticed the shops. The streets were lined with two story shop houses open to the streets with folding metal doors that some shopkeepers were now closing and locking in the evening darkness. Across the top of each shop a prominent sign proclaimed its name in both Thai and Chinese. We learned that people of Chinese descent dominated commerce in Thailand. There were shoe stores, food shops, clothe shops, motorcycle repair shops, every kind of shop seemingly without end for the entire drive into the city.

That evening we received an introduction to the wonderful restaurants of Bangkok. Our new friends took us to the Red Wall for dinner, a medium sized Chinese restaurant in a side street off of Suriwong Road. We sat around a round table on an open verandah and were handed cold towels to wipe our hands and face. The food came in several courses, consisting of a hot peppery soup, Pacific lobsters, sweet and sour pork, vegetable dishes and fragrant rice. It was a pleasant introduction to our new home.

After a few days in the Guest House, we moved into a small house in a *soi* (lane) off North Sathorn Road near a *klong* (canal) and watched Thailand unfold around us. It was a two story house with living room, dining room and kitchen on the first floor. Upstairs were two bedrooms and a bath. The house had electricity, cold running water, and the kitchen stove burned bottled gas. Similar sized houses were around us, some occupied by Thais and some by *farangs* (foreigners). On one side lived a middle aged New Zealander who worked for the New Zealand Embassy. She was the party lady. Perhaps she served as the official hostess for the embassy. Anyway, she had frequent, late and noisy parties. She employed a young Thai couple to help in her house. They had a son about the age of Lani, whose name was Lek. He and Lani became the best of friends and played together every day. Through them we got to know Lek's parents, who could speak some English, and other Thais in the lane.

One day we couldn't find Lani and went up and down the lane calling her name. A Thai woman, whom I had never seen before, came out of a yard and said, *"Lani doo teewee."* I didn't know what she was talking about until she pointed at the little house where Lek and his parents lived. I understood when I looked in the door and there were Lani and Lek watching television. We didn't have a television set, but they did. *"Doo teewee"* meant watching television. Every time we walked down the lane with Lani people we met would say, *"Lani pai nai?"* We soon learned that *"pai nai"* means "where are you going", and is a common greeting. Thai people love children and we discovered that walking with Lani was a good way to meet people. Lani responded to all greetings and after a few weeks was already picking up the language. Later, we were to wish that our own language learning would be so easy. Lani's transition to life in Thailand was easier than ours.

We had no air conditioning, which was true of most Thai houses at that time. Even though the weather was hot and humid Thai people preferred to sleep under mosquito nets without artificial cooling. Our house did have screens on the windows and heavy wooden shutters. We assumed the shutters were to close in case of rain, since there was no window glass. The first several nights in that house we went upstairs to bed leaving the downstairs shutters open. We thought it would be too hot to close them. A Thai neighbor came over one day and pointed to the shutters making closing motions and saying something that sounded like "*kamoy mak*." We had a complete communication gap and couldn't imagine what those words meant. I mentioned this to the Carders one day and they were horrified to learn that we had not been closing our downstairs shutters at night. "*Kamoy mak*" means many robbers!

We had only been in our house a few days when two young Thai women came to our door. They spoke to us in Thai. We spoke to them in English. No luck either way. Finally, one said in halting English, "We work for you, O.K.?" We would soon be starting Thai language school, Lani would need a baby sitter and Dee was six month pregnant. Those were all good reasons for having household help. Dee and I had discussed how we would interview applicants in an orderly fashion and select two that seemed best for us. Suddenly, these two young ladies, whom we had never seen before, had arrived ready to go to work. "Do you have any references?" I asked the one who had spoken English. Not understanding, she only shrugged her shoulders. Dee and I looked at one another, I shrugged my shoulders, and Dee said to the applicants, "You work for us, O.K.?" In this rather informal manner we acquired two sisters, Gee and Aroon. Gee established herself as cook and went to the fresh market every morning to buy food. Aroon cleaned the house and did our laundry. They breezed through the house in brisk efficiency, and soon became a part of the little society that lived on our lane. They could always be counted on to find Lani when she wandered off to play with children in the lane or watch television with Lek. They worked for us 18 months during our stay in Bangkok. Besides baby-sitting, keeping our clothes and house clean and food on the table, they helped us find our way into Thai life.

Lani, Rupert and Gee with a turkey we bought for
Thanksgiving dinner, 1963.

We also hired a man to take care of our yard and watch the house when we were gone. One day, without permission, he found the keys to a car we were using and took it for a drive. He didn't go far, just to the end of our *soi* and back to our house. Gee and Aroon, however, saw him do it and scolded him. Gee told him, "You will have to tell Mr. and Mrs. Nelson what you did." When Dee and I returned home the watchman sheepishly confessed that he had borrowed our car "for a short ride." Aroon was standing nearby to make sure he did tell us. Those two sisters were very responsible. We were fortunate to have them. We also learned that Thai women are strong, and take a major role in family life.

We found ourselves meeting new situations every day. One morning I walked out of our house and found our yard under water. The water was coming from the direction of the *klong*.

Our house was elevated about two feet off the ground, so the water flowed under the house and out the other side. Even the lane was covered, but people were wading through the water as if nothing had happened. No one was excited. The sun shone as brightly as ever. It had not rained, but there was the water flooding the whole neighborhood. I thought perhaps a dike had broken somewhere. The Gregory's lived across the *klong*, down Sathorn Road about five blocks, and in another *soi*. I hurried over to ask them what had happened, walking in water most of the way.

"Dick, where is all the water coming from?" I asked.

"What water?"

"This water all over. Our whole yard is flooded."

"Oh yeah, that's the high tide. Happens every year at this time."

"You mean it's not a flood?"

"Not really, it's just normal."

I was learning that "just normal" for Bangkok was not normal for South Dakota or Montana. I wasn't accustomed to that much water. I discovered that Bangkok has the highest tides of the year in November. At that time the Chao Phraya River, which flows through Bangkok, reaches its highest level because of rain runoff from the north. This high water corresponds to the high November tides causing the *klongs* to overflow and lower parts of the city are temporarily flooded. The Chao Phraya River originates in the northern mountains and drains the central plain of Thailand. Bangkok is only a few feet above sea level, thus the floods, which alarmed a dry-lander from the Northern Great Plains of North America.

The fact that Dee was expecting when we left the United States for Thailand added to our trepidation of moving to a land strange to us. Traveling half way around the world with a three year old daughter and a pregnant wife was an experience. I should have learned to ask, "Where's the toilet?" in a dozen languages before we started! We found an American doctor, Marshall Wells, at the Bangkok Christian Hospital to be Dee's doctor, and everything progressed well until she started getting a rash. This caused Dr. Wells some concern and he suggested that Dee see a specialist at Siriraj Hospital in Thonburi, across the Chao Phraya River from Bangkok.

Dr. Wells gave us a name, scribbled some directions on a scrap of paper and sent us on our way. We took a taxi to a ferry landing on the banks of the Chao Phraya and got into a water taxi jammed with people headed for Bangkok's sister city, Thonburi. Landing on the other side we walked several blocks to the hospital, which consisted of many buildings spread over a large campus. It took us some time to find the specialist. He was a Thai doctor who spoke fluent English. The medicine he prescribed for Dee soon cleared up her rash. However, she had to return several times for checkups.

It was a whole different world on the river. Strings of barges loaded with coconuts, bags of rice, timber or most anything were pulled up and down the river by sturdy little motor boats. Whole families lived on the blunt-nosed wooden barges. Bright colored ferry boats and water taxis, built long and narrow, darted about in all directions. Women in straw hats paddled small boats laden with fresh fruits and vegetables from which they peddled the produce. Small restaurant boats, just large enough for the woman owner and a charcoal stove, would stop along the bank whenever someone beckoned and sell bowls of noodles or grilled octopus. Sometimes the transaction took place mid-river with the occupants of another boat. Bangkok hasn't always had streets and roads. Formerly, transportation and commerce took place mostly along the river and *klongs*, and many of the old ways persisted in those places.

Floating market on a *klong*

One day we saw the Royal Barge out for a practice run. The Royal Barge is a special boat carved from a single teak log and used to transport His Majesty the King during rare ceremonial occasions on the river. It was a long narrow boat with a giant mythical animal's head on the prow. The brilliant red tunics of the oarsmen glittered in the sun as they lifted the forty golden paddles, like a swan spreading her wings, in unison to the beat of a drum. The golden throne for His Majesty was placed in the center of the boat. The boatmen maneuvered down the river with the ancient Khmer towers of the Temple of the Dawn in the background. The sight took our breath away.

Wat Arun (Temple of the Dawn).

One night, about three weeks before our baby was due to arrive, I went to teach English at the Maitrijit Chinese Church night school. That class had been established to help young men and women learn English, and so help them advance in their careers and businesses. I was glad to find something useful to do that brought me into contact with Thai people. In this case, Thai of Chinese descent. I taught two nights a week. On that particular night Dee was feeling rather uncomfortable when I left, so I hurried home right after the class. I found her in even greater discomfort, and having stomach pains.

We had no phone, but Dee thought I had better call Dr. Lewis and consult with him, so late at night I walked down our lane to Sathorn Road, crossed over the *klong* and into the lane where the Gregories lived to use their phone. Their house was closed and dark.

"Dick, are you home?" I yelled as I knocked on the door.

"Yes, who is it?" came a muffled voice from inside.

"It's me, Rupert. May I use your telephone?"

"Yes, I guess so. Come on in."

9

"The door is locked."

"Oh yeah, just a minute."

I heard the sound of sliding door bolts and the door swung open. Dick stood in the doorway in a pair of loose Chinese pajamas.

"I have to call Dr. Wells about Dee," I blurted out.

"Oh, is the baby coming already?" Marnie's voice came from the bedroom.

"No, no," I replied. "She's just not feeling well tonight."

Dr. Wells and his wife lived next to the hospital. He had given us his home phone number just in case we needed it, so I called that number. It was about 1:00 A.M. After several rings he answered. He sounded sleepy and a bit grumpy.

"Dee's not feeling well," I informed him.

"Well, what's the matter?"

"She's having stomach pains and seems restless."

"Well, she is pregnant you know."

"Yes, I know."

"Does there seem to be any regularity to the pains, or are they constant?" the doctor wanted to know.

"Gee, I don't know. She just said she had stomach pains."

"Well, it's three weeks yet before the baby is due, so it's probably just the Bangkok belly."

"Yeah, I think that's it." I replied with a sense of relief.

I thanked Dick for the use of his telephone and wearily walked back home. "Don't worry," I informed Dee, "It's just the Bangkok belly. Let's go to bed." However, Dee continued to be restless, and kept complaining about pains, which were coming more frequently. I was having a hard time getting to sleep. Finally, Dee sat up in bed and announced, "You had better get me to the hospital right now unless you want to deliver this baby yourself." That, I didn't want to do.

We had recently been provided with a Volkswagen Beetle that was normally used by someone else in the Mission. Cecil Carder had said, "You had better have it just in case." The "just in case" had happened. I dressed again, helped Dee into the car and drove down the dark, deserted streets to Bangkok Christian Hospital on Silom Road. The delivery room and maternity ward were located on the second floor of one of the buildings and we had to climb an outside staircase. Dee made it up the stairs and the Thai nurses took charge.

One of those nurses helped Dee on to an examining table, took one look and said, "*Riak maw, reo reo.*" (Call the doctor quickly). By the time Dr. Wells arrived, in his bedroom slippers, the baby was on its way. We had a new daughter 30 minutes after arriving at the hospital. Neither Dr. Wells nor I mentioned the stomach ache diagnosis that we had arrived at over the telephone. I drove back home alone, and thankfully, crawled into a quiet bed.

The following morning I sat with Dee in her hospital room thinking of names for girls. Mrs. Wells, who was a nurse at the hospital, came along and said she always liked the name, Rebecca. We did too, so settled on Rebecca Ruth. She came three weeks early, didn't eat much for a few days, but as Dr. Wells said, "Any baby that cries that loud is plenty healthy." Now we had all arrived in Thailand.

Dee and Rebecca when she was a few weeks old.

LANGUAGE STUDY

"A different language is a different vision of life." Federico Fellini

We expected to live in Thailand for several years, so our first assignment was to learn the language. This was considered so very important that fifteen months were given for that task. We had no other work to do, only language study.

Like most Americans, I was monolingual. English was my only language. My mother and father were born in the United States, but their parents were immigrants from Denmark. My parents spoke Danish in their homes as children, and when I was a boy, they would speak some Danish with their old friends. I never learned more than a handful of the most commonly used words. I recall being very frustrated listening to stories when those friends came visiting. The entire story would be told in English and I would listen avidly as the story developed. More often than not, however, the punch line would be given in Danish. Everybody would laugh uproariously, and ignore my urgent question, "What did he say?" Finally, someone would reply, "It only makes sense in Danish." I never could understand why what was said in one language couldn't be said just as well in another. When I became a little older, I suspected the part in Danish was for the benefit of my young and tender ears.

Dee is a third generation American, just as I am, but the native language tradition had persisted longer in her family. Chinese was used in her home when she was a child, and as an adult she could still understand the Cantonese dialect. She tried to teach me, but I proved to be a hopeless student. Of course, being met with peals of laughter every time I attempted to say something didn't exactly encourage me.

We arrived in Bangkok a few weeks too late to immediately start on our Thai language course at the Union Language School on Sathorn Road. We had to wait about two months until a new class started. Most Thai people did not speak English, so we were constantly frustrated by our inability to communicate with the people around us. It was even worse than missing the punch line of old Danish jokes!

Finally, one Monday morning Dee and I were part of a group of six *Farangs* grouped around a table with a Thai woman teacher. She announced that her name was Khru Prida. "My first name is Prida, but *khru* means teacher, so you must always address me as Khru Prida. I have a last name, but that is not important. In Thailand we use first names." She went on to explain that she would address us by our first names, preceded by the word *khun*. *Khun* is a polite title, like Mr. or Mrs., that can be used with anyone, except children or royalty. In the class we became "Khun Rupert" and "Khun Dee."

We met in the upstairs of a spacious old wooden building on North Sathorn Road. Many other classes, such as ours, were meeting in various parts of the building, so there was a constant hum of voices. Fans vibrated from the ceiling, moving the musty, warm air around. We had four classes each morning, each taught by a different teacher, but Khru Prida was responsible for our progress. We were given lesson sheets every day with sentence patterns and vocabulary to learn. Those were written in a Romanized phonetic system, so we could read the Thai words and learn to pronounce them. Reading Thai letters would come later. The teachers lead us in endless drills and practice of the vocabulary. By mid-morning the room was uncomfortably hot, and when we finished at noon we were exhausted. However, the day's studies were not over. We found we had to study at least four hours at home in order to keep up in class. We were expected to know our vocabulary each day. Khru Prida was a good teacher willing to help us in anyway she could, but she also had a sharp tongue which she didn't hesitate to aim at a lagging student. One day I did not know my vocabulary. She soon noticed.

"Khun Rupert, what were you doing last night?"

"I was tired," was my feeble reply.

"Do you think I get tired sometimes?"

"Yes, I'm sure you do."

"The Language School pays my salary. Even if I'm tired I must still prepare. Who pays your salary Khun Rupert?"

"The Baptist Mission pays my salary."

"Well, yesterday they did not get their moneys worth. Tomorrow I trust you will come prepared."

"Yes, Khru Prida."

I did come prepared the next day. I tried to come to class prepared every day even if it required studying late at night.

Thai is a tonal language and we English speakers found that characteristic difficult to master. Many words or syllables sounded alike to us at first, but actually they had totally different meanings according to the tone, or pitch, of one's voice. Thai has five tones, so one similar sound could have five different meanings, depending on if you gave it a high, low, mid, rising or falling pitch. We were soon confused and dismayed by our task, and began to wonder if it was possible to learn such a language. Every morning, however, Khru Prida would greet us in Thai and wait for a reply. She would ask simple questions, always knowing how much vocabulary we should have learned, and stand there waiting for a reply, which we must give in Thai. She never allowed us any excuse and never failed to correct a mispronounced word. She had great patience.

Our daughter, Rebecca, was born the night following our first day of language study. Dee said, "I didn't know Thai study would have that kind of affect on me!" Dee missed a few days of school, but soon one of the teachers came to our house two hours a day to teach her. She was soon progressing nearly as fast as the rest of us. A tonal language was not new to Dee. Her Cantonese dialect has nine tones.

We studied the Thai language for fifteen months, and I think that was the most difficult time of my life. We were not only studying intensely, but also having to adjust to a different life style and a different climate. Also, Rebecca demanded her share of attention. Thai women love babies, so Gee and Aroon fussed over her and carried her around all day. At night, when Gee and Aroon had left, Rebecca expected the same treatment from us. She would go to sleep about 9:00 every night, and we would carefully lay her in her crib, where she would sleep soundly for all of five minutes. Suddenly, she would wake up screaming, and continue screaming until picked up. It wasn't good enough just to pick her up, however, you also had to walk her. No standing in one place. No rocking in a rocking chair. Only walking would do. After a long time, she would again fall asleep and we would carefully lay her in her crib. If we were lucky, she would sleep out what remained of the night. If not, we carried her again. One night Dee and I decided to let her cry. Surely, she would go to sleep eventually, and break herself of that habit. After several hours of screaming, we gave in and walked her again. Since our upstairs shutters were always open, Becky kept the whole *soi* awake that night. Several neighbors asked about Rebecca the following day, so we decided that "letting her cry it out," was not a viable solution.

So we studied eight hours a day; spent some time with Lani, and carried Rebecca at night. All of that in the humid heat of equatorial Bangkok while adjusting to the lack of telephones, strange food, and new customs. We were also bothered by mosquitoes. The walls of our house had cracks that made it possible for them to enter. We slept under mosquito nets, but Lani wiggled around in her bed at night which opened the net and allowed in mosquitoes. Before I went to bed I checked on her and there were always mosquitoes biting her. She would also be perspiring profusely. I killed those mosquitoes, but knew that more would be biting her before morning. I hit an emotional low one evening when I took Lani for a walk around the streets near our house. We sat to rest on a tree stump for a few minutes, not realizing it was the home of stinging ants. Lani was badly bitten and had red welts on her legs. I felt I had made a big mistake taking her to a place where her pajamas were wet with perspiration every morning and where I couldn't even protect her against mosquitoes and ants.

We were not the only ones to experience culture shock and despair of ever learning the language. Sometimes a fellow student would fail to appear in class. Later, we would learn that person had decided to go home, never to return. We learned that the ability to learn a language has nothing to do with previous academic achievement. I saw men with an earned doctorate nearly reduced to tears at their fumbling attempts to speak, while someone with scarcely any education beyond high school made fantastic progress. People who felt too dignified to make errors had the hardest time. Those who went around speaking what they knew, no matter how atrociously, laughing at their errors and trying again, were the ones who progressed.

Khru Prida, and the other teachers, not only taught a language, but also Thai customs and way of life. We learned, for example, of Thai customs pertaining to the feet and to the head. One day Khru Prida walked into our classroom to find some of us with our feet on the table.

"Please put your feet on the floor," she said, "It is not polite."

"But it's so hot today," we grumbled.

"Do you want to live in Thailand with *Farangs* or with Thai?"

"With Thai."

"You can't live with Thai people if your feet are on the table."

"What's feet got to do with it?"

"In Thailand," Khru Prida explained, "the feet are considered the lowest part of the body. They tread in the dirt and dust and are not to be prominently shown. When you sit, keep your feet under you. Never use your feet for pointing, or anything that draws attention to them."

When Khru Prida spoke in her quiet, but intense tone of voice, we knew it was important, and we listened. She went on to tell about the head.

"The head is the most elevated part of the body, not just by its physical location, but also in our social customs. Never touch a Thai person on the head. If you must reach over a Thai, always pause and excuse yourself first."

Day by day we learned. We learned not only a language, but a culture. We learned that much culture is learned only through the language. We learned that there are many titles besides "Khru" and "Khun", and that one's social rank, especially if you are a Thai, affects your use of language when speaking to others of varying social rank. As words began to come together, our understanding of Thai people also came together and life began to take on more meaning, and we lost many of our former frustrations. S h o p p i n g expeditions became fun when we learned to bargain and ask questions of the shopkeepers. "How much is this mango?" I would ask.

"Ten Baht."

"Oh, that's very expensive. I'll give you four Baht."

"At four Baht I'll lose money. How about eight Baht?"

"I'll give you five Baht and that's all."

"OK, OK. For a *Farang* you are a good bargainer. How long have you lived in Thailand?"

"One year."

"Only one year! You speak Thai very well. You must be very smart."

An ego bolstering conversation like that could be most encouraging. Naturally, I always returned to make additional purchases from that shop, even when Gee told me I shouldn't pay more than three Baht for a mango.

We began to enter into the little society in our *soi*, and learned all kinds of fascinating tidbits that had not been accessible to us before. Imagine, we had lived in that *soi* for a whole year and never knew that Lek's mother had an operation so she couldn't have any more babies. We learned that Aroon, who had six children, wanted such an operation, but her husband wouldn't agree. We learned that the young wife of a gardener at a house down the soi was really his *mia noi* (minor wife).

"Where's his major wife?" I asked Aroon.

"Oh, she's upcountry in his home province."

"Does she know about her husband's second wife?"

"No. She's far away."

"Does he ever go home?"

"Sometimes, but not often. He has a family to care for here now."

One Thai woman on the soi had a baby every year. Her husband was a cheerful fellow, but he drank a lot. When he was sober, he worked on construction jobs and would turn his earnings over to his wife. When he drank, he spent all his money and came home to sleep. One day we were informed by Aroon that this lady would have no more babies. "How can that be?" I asked. "Did she have an operation?"

"No, but she sent her husband to have one. That works too, you know, and besides, it's cheaper that way."

A few months later we came home to find this man's wife complaining loudly to Gee and Aroon about her husband.

"That man is good for only one thing."

"What's that?" Gee asked with a sly grin.

"You know he puts a baby in my stomach every year, and now he's done it again."

"I thought you sent him to have an operation?"

"I did, but that son of a monkey spent the money I gave him on whiskey and never told me. He hasn't been near a doctor, but he'll sure need one if he comes home tonight." Life on our soi was never this interesting before.

There are many pitfalls in the Thai language to cause the unwary *Farang* embarrassing mistakes. Besides changing voice tones, each vowel can be either long or short, making totally different words. For example, the word *bot* with a short "o" vowel means chapter, but with a long vowel it means a temple building or church. In addition, every noun must have a classifier, which appears only at the end of a sentence. You must learn which classifiers go with which nouns. These give further meaning to the noun and the number is attached to the classifier. For example, in English we would say, "I have five oranges", but in Thai it is, "I have oranges five *bai.*" In this case *bai* is the classifier for various kinds of round objects.

I once made a bad mistake involving classifiers. Lani was attending a Thai kindergarten that was owned by a Thai princess. It was a good school with a highly educated staff. One day I went to the school to pay Lani's fees, and met the principal. She spoke excellent English, but Khru Prida had told us to always practice our Thai in real life situations. I summoned up my courage and came up with a question that was quite disconnected with our previous English conversation. I asked in my best Thai, "How many students do you have in this school?" Khru Prida would have been proud of my sentence construction. I think I even had the tones reasonably correct. However, I used the classifier for animals, so what I actually said was, "In this school you have students how many animals?" The principal replied without any hesitation, although I noticed an odd twitch in her facial muscles, as she repressed her laughter. My mistake didn't occur to me until I returned home. I avoided the kindergarten for some time after that. In Thai society it is considered very impolite to cause someone else to lose face. In that situation the principal took heroic measures to avoid laughing, which would make me lose face.

During our period of study at the Union Language School, a supposedly true story was being told about a *Farang* lady who had lived in Bangkok for several years. She enjoyed horseback riding and was very pleased to find the Bangkok Polo Club, where she could ride early in the morning. In great excitement she told her Thai neighbor how much she enjoyed horseback riding every morning. Unfortunately, the words for ride and feces are very close, being only a tonal difference. What she said was, "I enjoy horse manure every morning." Undoubtedly, we foreigners kept the Thai population amused.

A doctor friend started examining patients at the Bangkok Christian Hospital while he was still at language school. One day he was examining a young lady. "Do you have a cough?" he asked. The only difference between the Thai words for cough and shy is the vowel length. Naturally, he used the wrong one and asked the bewildered girl if she was shy. I've often wondered what she thought the doctor was going to do next! Her ordeal wasn't over yet. "Stick out your tongue," he said. Confusing the two words, he actually asked her to "stick out her drawer." Anyway, that experience motivated the doctor to apply himself with greater diligence to his lessons.

The words for cross and trousers also sound similar in *Farang* ears and are often confused. Many aspiring young missionaries have preached eloquent sermons to puzzled congregations on the subject of the "The Old Wooden Trousers!"

Undoubtedly, I made many similar mistakes which never became known to me. Because of Thai politeness, mistakes made in public usually went uncorrected. Khru Prida, however, never failed to let you know of mispronunciations, and made us repeat it correctly to her satisfaction.

Children learn languages much easier than adults. We noticed that Lani and Rebecca just absorbed the language. They spoke it correctly, tones and all. With no effort they could switch from one language to another, speaking Thai to a Thai person and English to a Westerner. Oh, that our own language learning was so easy.

At that time in the Thai school system nationwide comprehensive examinations were given all students following the fourth grade, seventh grade, tenth grade, and twelfth grade. In the rural villages many students dropped out of school after the fourth or seventh grade. Foreigners teaching in Thai schools were supposed to pass the fourth grade exam as evidence of an ability to comprehend, speak, read and write the Thai language. Dee and I decided to take the exam as our formal language study drew to a close. I didn't plan to teach in a school, but Dee had already been asked to do some English teaching.

Khru Prida took charge of a cramming course, as if preparing us for university finals. After coaching us through a month of extra study, she accompanied us to the Marble Temple, where the exam was given. An assortment of about twenty *Farangs* showed up for the exam. Unlike regular fourth graders, we did not have to be examined in arithmetic, and all the various school subjects. This was a special exam developed by the Ministry of Education solely to test ability in the Thai language. The exam lasted from 8:00 A.M. until noon and was divided into four parts. We each had to converse with one of the examiners to test our ability in conversational Thai. Next, we had to write a short essay in Thai on a subject that was given us. Thirdly, we were given some printed material to read and then tested on the material to determine our reading comprehension. Finally, a story was read to us and we were tested on our oral comprehension.

The following day Khru Prida interrogated us about the content of the exam, and waited as impatiently as we did for the results. Dee and I received our notice through the mail, but Khru Prida already knew. She had traveled across town to the Ministry of Education building as soon as the results were posted. We both had passed, and Khru Prida's beaming face was our reward.

For one year and three months we had sweated and struggled, moaned and groaned our way through our daily lessons. Now Khru Prida was ready to push us out to make room for new students.

"Congratulations, Khun Rupert and Khun Dee. You passed the exam."

"Thank you."

"You have only begun to learn the Thai language, but you have started. Now you must continue learning for as long as you live in Thailand."

"Oh, Khru Prida, I am tired of studying," I protested.

"Not everything is learned from books. Now you must listen to Thai people. When you hear a new word, find out its meaning."

And so we graduated from the Union Language School, with Khru Prida's stern admonition ringing in our ears. I now understand why some things only make sense in Thai.

BANGKOK EVENTS

In the more urbanized and affluent parts of Thailand, particularly Bangkok, rumors and gossip about high government officials and well known personalities were always making the rounds. From society matrons to noodle vendors, one could always pick up a bit of information about some well known personality.

During our period of language study, Prime Minister Sarit became very ill with a liver condition from which he never recovered. His illness, although not mentioned in the newspapers, had been the topic of much discussion for some time, and anyone who had Thai acquaintances were told quite cheerfully about Prime Minister Sarit's excessive drinking and womanizing. Some people admired him for his refusal to surrender to the needs of his liver, but to keep going full blast nearly to the end.

The censored newspapers and radio were silent on the subject of Sarit's approaching death, but everyone knew it was coming, and this brought out coup rumors. Governments often changed by coups in Thailand, especially upon the demise of a strong man like Sarit.

During that time, one of my languages classes was newspaper reading. To obtain a Thai newspaper I would walk on a narrow footpath along the banks of a *klong* and on to the busy commercial street of Silom Road. I always bought my copy of "Siam Rath" from the same newslady who had a little stand next to the Siam Commercial Bank. We would exchange a few words, as I wanted to practice my classroom Thai in "real life" situations. She came to recognize me and would ask the usual questions. "Did I like Thailand?" "Did I like Thai girls?" "What was my salary?" One day during the Sarit illness, I asked her about his condition. She told me in confidential tones, *"Sarit tai laew"* (already dead). She went on to explain that the big men in the government didn't want to disclose this yet in order to prevent a coup. She said, "You buy lots of food. Fill all your water pots. Lots of trouble coming. Stores closed. Water cut off."

Somewhat disturbed, I hurried home and told Dee what I had heard. We had no previous experience in such matters, so decided to ask the opinion of the two Thai people who were closest to us, Gee and Aroon, the two sisters who worked for us. They had already heard the rumors, but were sure there would be no trouble. *"Sarit tai laew,* but never mind, there will be no trouble."

"Maybe we should buy extra food and fill water jugs just in case," I argued.

"No need, no need," replied Aroon. "I have a friend who works for a big man in the government. She says no trouble."

As the rumors of an impending coup became more serious, other Westerners sought advice from their respective embassies. Long time residents of Thailand advised us to stock up on food and water. Armchair political scientists predicted a severe political struggle was shaping up.

We, however, did nothing. After all, our own impeccable sources had informed us that Sarit was indeed dead but that there would be no coup. Within a few days it was announced by newspapers and radio that Prime Minister Sarit had died and a new government was already formed. The crisis was over and everything returned to normal. How two servants knew all that I'll never know. That's Thailand.

Prior to beginning our work in Thailand, we had attended orientation courses on Thailand, Southeast Asian studies, linguistic studies, and I had read everything I could find about Thai agriculture. One thing that was omitted, however, was a course on the care and feeding of visitors. Bangkok was a favorite tourist location, so people were always coming through who wanted to see Bangkok "as it really is." They also liked to go shopping, so we would take them to the lacquer ware shops, jewelry stores, silk shops, and wood carving shops. One salesgirl saw me so often she asked me for what travel agency I worked!

Toward the end of our language study in Bangkok a group of church women from South Dakota came through to "get a first hand look" at Thailand. Dee and I took the group to, Mahachai, a Chinese fishing town on the Gulf of Siam. There was a small Christian community there and some of those people took us on a tour of a local industry, which was a processing plant where fish were converted to *nampla* (fish sauce) in smelly, concrete tanks. There was a general murmur of approval when our guide announced we would next take a ride on a fishing boat. Smelling rotten fish does get old after a while.

Our boat was just approaching the dock when we arrived. Most of our group waited patiently on the dock, but one of the Dakota ladies was not going to stand idle. As soon as the boat reached the end of the dock, she started to climb on board. The dock was low and the boat rather high. There was a ledge all around the outside of the boat onto which she stepped and grasped onto a convenient handhold above her head. However, she couldn't climb on up the side of the hull and didn't know where to go from there. The fishermen on the boat didn't realize one passenger was attempting to board, but they realized the position of the boat was inconvenient, so they opened the throttle and moved away from the dock to make a wide circle, so as to approach the dock from a better position for boarding.

25

They appeared to be going back out to sea. One of my most vivid memories is seeing that seventy year old widow lady from Deadwood, South Dakota, hanging on to the outside of a Thai fishing boat as it maneuvered around in the Gulf of Siam. Upon the return of the boat, she nonchalantly stepped back on to the dock and waited to board with the rest of us in a more orthodox fashion. They make 'em tough in Deadwood. After all, that was the home of Calamity Jane!

Our time in Bangkok was not always enjoyable. The weather was hot and humid. The traffic was bad. We had a new baby while living far from home. Went through culture shock, and spent most of our days in language study. Still, it was a fascinating city with a blend of the old Siam and the new Thailand. It was our entry to Thailand and all the experiences that were to follow.

THE RIVER KWAI

One hot afternoon while we were still in language school, Cecil Carder came by to see me at our house. "Want to go on a trip?" he asked.

"Sure. Where are we going?"

"Up the Kwai River to Sangklaburi. I have to go anyway, and thought you might want to go along."

"I sure do! When do we leave?"

"Day after tomorrow."

I had read about the "Death Railway" and seen the movie "Bridge on The River Kwai," so I was eager to go for a first hand look. I would have to play hooky from language school for a few days, but I reasoned a little vacation would do me good. I'm not a city person and I was eager to get out of Bangkok.

During World War II Allied prisoners of war, captured by the Japanese, were forced to build a railroad from near Bangkok to Moulmein, Burma. Most of those men were captured when Singapore, Malaysia, Indonesia, and Hong Kong fell to the advancing Japanese armies. They were mostly English, Australian, and Dutch. Thousands of Asians were also forced to work on the railroad.

The railroad was important to the Japanese, as they intended to use it to move men and supplies over it in their struggle to capture Burma and India. The fighting in that part of the world was a backwash of the global war and did not receive much attention from American war correspondents. Little was known of the men who suffered and died to build that railroad.

The railroad was about four hundred miles long, and its construction cost the lives of nearly two hundred men per mile. They died from disease, starvation, overwork, and from despair. The railroad crossed mountains, rivers, swamps, and jungles. Much of the way it followed a river: The River Kwai. The Thai railroad system still uses part of the track, but farther up country, near Burma, the rails have been torn up and the jungle has reclaimed its own. We would have to travel most of the way by boat. The famous bridge built by the prisoners of war was located near where we started our trip.

Dick Gregory took Cecil and me to the town of Kanchanaburi, where we would catch a train for the first leg of our trip. It was a two hour ride. First we went through rice fields, then as the land became hillier, through sugar cane. The sharp acrid stink of sugar processing plants clung to our nostrils for several miles after passing them.

Kanchanaburi had the look of a frontier town, or a mining town. Raw, unfinished, crude, but hard working. Unpainted wooden houses on the edge of town gave way to two-story cement stucco buildings in the business center. Several of those buildings were still under construction, with bamboo scaffolding flimsily attached to them. The completed buildings contained a variety of shops and businesses, not unlike the shop rows in Bangkok. These, however, reflecting their more rural setting, had more shops containing farming equipment, fertilizer, and the various needs of the rural villagers. We made a brief stop at the fresh produce market and Cecil purchased some dried bananas to eat on our trip. We continued on to the train station just on the other side of town. Cecil had made this trip before and said the train was due at 10:40 A.M., but was rather irregular. "What time is the train coming today?" Cecil asked the ticket agent.

"What train?"

"The train to Wangpo."

"Well, it's due at 10:40."

"I know, but will it be on time today?"

"No."

"What time will it come?"

"It'll be at least one hour late, and if it doesn't come then, it will this afternoon."

At least it was likely to come, so we bought our tickets to Wangpo and told the agent we would go and eat lunch and come back later. Wangpo is nearly at the end of the line. Beyond Wangpo we would travel by boat. We had packed some sandwiches from Bangkok, so went to the site of the Bridge Over The River Kwai to eat a picnic lunch. I was somewhat disappointed to see that all traces of the wooden bridge built by the prisoners had disappeared. Nearby, was a more permanent bridge now in use.

After eating, we drove on to a nearby memorial cemetery where remains of some of the prisoners are buried. I was impressed by how neatly it was maintained, but it had an aura of foreignness about it, as though the closely kept lawns belonged in an English park rather than clipped out of the jungle on the banks of a swirling, chocolate brown river. It seemed to me the bodies interred here remained as strange to this place as when they had labored and died twenty years earlier. Each marker had an inscription engraved on it as requested by the family of the deceased. Two markers caught my eye as we walked in the cemetery.

"Private T. E. Whetton
The Leicestershire Regt.
24th August 1944 Age 45
His heart true and tender.
Always did his best and left us to remember.
Wife, Children."

"Driver L. Singer
Royal Signals
18th Oct. 1943 Age 36
In memory of a dear husband and
loving father. Always in our thoughts."

In a rather subdued mood we returned to the train station, just in time to hear the whistle of the incoming train. I hadn't heard a whistle like that for a long time. The engine was an old wood-burning steam engine. When I was a boy, the sound of such whistles used to echo across the South Dakota prairies reaching into my upstairs bedroom at night calling me to far places.

Steam engine train at Kanchanaburi.

Cecil went up into a car first. I handed our baggage to him through an open window and climbed aboard. The train chugged out of the station at 12:00 noon, and almost immediately rattled across the new railroad bridge where we had eaten our lunch. We continued along the Valley of the Kwai. Sometimes the tracks were laid on a trestle alongside a sheer cliff dropping straight down to the river. At other times we passed through sugar cane fields, their white plumes waving in a gentle breeze. Gradually, the cultivated areas decreased as the land became hillier and covered with green jungle vegetation.

The coach seats were wooden benches with vertical backs facing one another. This arrangement placed each passenger in a close relationship with those sitting opposite. A family of three children and their mother were opposite us. The youngest must have been about a year old. She sat quietly on her mother's lap. The other two were boys about three and five. They had been playing in the aisle, but when we sat down, they ran to their mother. Clinging to her long skirt, they turned and looked at us with apprehensive eyes. The baby began to cry and her mother offered her a breast, which she slurped at noisily, occasionally rolling her eyes around to look at us. I took out a package of gum and slowly opened it, with the two boys watching every move. I removed two sticks and handed them to the boys. Two grubby, hesitant hands slowly came up and took the gum. "Say thank you," said the mother, as mothers do around the world. The two boys raised their hands in a *wai* (curtsy) and said *kopjai* (thanks).

Pai nai ma?" (Where are you coming from?) Cecil asked.

"From Bangkok," replied the mother with a smile. Surprised to find we spoke Thai.

"Do you live there?"

"No, we live in Wangpo, but my husband is working in Bangkok. We have been to see him."

"Now you're going home?"

"Yes, it costs too much to live in Bangkok. We cannot afford to live there."

Two men sitting across the aisle from us now joined in.

"Yes, Bangkok is too expensive," said one. "You have to rent a house and buy food. It's too much. It's better to live in a small town."

"But can you find work in a small town?" piped in the other man. "Look at me. I am a carpenter, but not much work for me here."

Eighty percent of Thailand's people still lived in rural areas, but farms were small and there was a great desire to find additional work.

"How much do you make a day?" I asked the carpenter.

"Around here I make thirty Baht ($1.50). In Bangkok twice that much."

"Do you have a family?"

"Yes, I have a wife and four children. I used to work in Bangkok too, but I'd sooner work near home."

"Is thirty Baht enough?"

"No, my family can't live on that. Sometimes my wife works on construction jobs. She gets only fifteen Baht a day. We have a garden and raise some pigs. We get along."

The train pulled into a station and some vendors came on the train. One boy, about twelve years old, was the first into our car. He had several plastic bags containing a black liquid looped over his arm. *"Oliang, oliang"* he chanted as he walked down the aisle. Eager hands reached out for the bags of iced black coffee and soon they were gone. A straw stuck in each bag makes a convenient container for any kind of drink.

Next, a little girl came by selling sugar cane. She had the stalks peeled and cut into sections about one inch long. Each section was stuck on a bamboo skewer. She held a handful like a bouquet of yellow dandelions. "Ten pieces for one baht." Not bad. That's only five cents. She also had bags of peanuts boiled in the shell and still hot. I bought a bag for a baht. A large lady wearing a sarong and the distinctive straw hat worn by farm women in central Thailand came with a large basket of fruit. She had hairy red rambutans, green shiny guavas, purple mangosteens, and custard apples. Cecil bought some rambutans, but I settled for two custard apples. They are not really apples, but are a fruit with a bumpy green skin. Inside, numerous black seeds are imbedded in the white custard-like flesh. I enjoyed sitting next to the open window and spitting out the seeds as we rattled along.

After a three hour trip, we arrived in Wangpo, and unloaded in great confusion. Wangpo is on the Kwai River and has a boat dock, so people continuing on by boat got off there. Several boatmen were trying to get passengers for their boats. Women pushing two-wheeled carts offered to take our luggage to the boat docks. Dr. Corpron, a missionary doctor at Sangklaburi, knew we were coming, so had sent his boatman, Wate, to meet us. It was too late in the day to start now, so we hired a woman with a push cart to take our luggage to the hotel. It was more than we could carry, as we also had some supplies for the hospital.

I'm sure that hotel has never been recommended in any travel guide books. It was an unpainted two-story wooden structure. The first floor, open on two sides, contained a restaurant. Rooms were upstairs. Cecil and I got one with two single beds. There was no ceiling fan. In fact, there was no electricity during the day time. The heat in our room was unbearable, so we went back downstairs and each had a bottle of soda pop cooled in a kerosene refrigerator.

Wate had just finished repairing his boat and wanted to check it out, so we went with him to the docks. Wate had a dark complexion with an easy smile. He wore a long *pakama* (loin cloth) and his long, black hair hung down from under his straw hat. We had to go down a steep embankment to the river. Alongside the crumbling cement steps were two cable car tracks. A small car was on each track, so arranged that when one car went down, the other car went up. A gasoline engine powered the cable car which was used to load and unload freight. There were a number of villages upstream accessible only by the river boats.

Along the river were several floating rafts, on which were houses, restaurants, and shops. About twenty long, narrow boats were tied to those floating docks. We climbed into Wate's boat and took a trial run upstream for about five minutes. The engine ran perfectly. These boats are called *hangyao* (long tail). They can be any length, but Wate's boat was about twenty feet long and just wide enough for two rather small people to sit side by side. They use an outboard engine with the propeller on the end of a long shaft extending out the rear of the boat. This shaft is maneuverable and can be raised to go over shallow water or turned to steer the boat. The boat had no roof, so on the way back to the hotel we bought straw hats to wear the following day.

We needed a bath by the time we got back to the hotel and found the bathroom down the hall from our room. We bathed by dipping water from a large crock. Refreshed, we went down to see what culinary adventures awaited us in the restaurant. We were not surprised to discover a somewhat limited menu, so we settled for *kutio pat* (fried rice noodles) with beef and green vegetables. At dusk a diesel generator started up and the lights came on. Cecil and I read in bed for a while, but too many bugs were attracted to the light. One huge black specimen caromed around the room like a flying toy tank banging into walls and ceiling. We finally turned off the lights and went to bed. The mattresses were two-inch thick kapok-filled pads over bed slats. A confused rooster in a pen below our open window kept crowing all night. All in all, I was rather glad when morning came.

We ate a quick breakfast of boiled duck eggs and ovaltine at the same restaurant, and walked to the river front where we loaded our belongings in the boat and took off upstream. The noise of the boat engine made conversation difficult, so I just sat and watched the passing sights from my vantage point in the prow of the boat. In most places the jungle and bamboo forest came right to the river's edge. Rice fields or orchards would appear as we neared an occasional village, only to give way to the jungle again as we proceeded. Further back, rimming the valley, were emerald green mountains shimmering in the fresh morning sun. Frequently, we would see elephants working along the bank, dragging logs or bamboo poles to be made into rafts and floated downstream to sell. Bright colored birds of red, green, yellow and blue flitted along the banks. Once, a great hornbill flew across the river nearly over our boat. Those large birds have huge yellow beaks, and fly as if they haven't quite mastered the art of keeping airborne. We had to stop once to change the propeller and again to clean the gas filter in the boat engine. All of this delayed us about two hours.

We came to the small town of Takanun at 3:30. The name of this town means "jackfruit landing." Cecil thought we should stay there overnight because our delays had made it impossible to make it to Sangklaburi before dark. However, Wate assured us it would be safe to travel after dark because there was less traffic farther upstream. We loaded up on gasoline, and I bought bananas and pomelo, a fruit similar to grapefruit. From there on the river narrowed, but the current was faster. We saw several waterfalls along the bank where smaller streams emptied into the Kwai. I came to appreciate Wate's skill in judging which side of the river to take to avoid sandbars and submerged rocks or logs. Occasionally, we came to rapids which seemed impossible to navigate, but Wate would head into them at just the right position and open the throttle wide. The boat would hesitate for a second and then plunge up the rapids, narrowly avoiding rocks on both sides of the boat. Sometimes the water would spray into the boat soaking us in its delicious coolness. Once I looked back at Wate and he flashed a big smile, as if to say, "Don't worry, we'll make it."

It was dark by about 6:00 o'clock. Wate slowed down, but we kept going. He seemed to know every inch of the river. Cecil and I found our flashlights in our luggage and used them to spot the banks and rocks. I think Wate could have made it without our help, but it made us feel better. Fireflies swarmed along the banks, relieving the darkness with their intermittent flashing.

I was conscious of coming to a fork in the river, and after that the channel became much smaller. I remembered seeing on a map where three small rivers come together to form the Kwai near Sangklaburi, so I knew we were close to our destination. At one point we all had to get out to pull the boat over a shallow place. Now that the sun had gone down the cold water made me shiver. Finally, we turned a bend and there were the welcome lights of the Corpron residence. It was 7:30. We had been on the river for twelve hours. We clomped up the bank with stiff legs to the Corpron home, where Mrs. Corpron had dinner waiting.

After dinner my tiredness must have been apparent. Doug took me to my sleeping place, which was a cot in a screened in porch. My last memories of that day were listening to the call of a *tokae* lizard in a tree just outside the screen. This lizard starts out making a sound like someone clearing their throat and then calls its name several times. *"Tokae, tokae, tokae"*. I've heard Thai people say, "If the *Tokae* calls its name nine times that is good luck, so go out and buy a lottery ticket."

SANGKLABURI

I woke up to the smell of breakfast cooking and quickly dressed to go out and learn more about this place.   Two American families lived at this station, but Paul and Winnie Dodge were on home leave, so the Corprons were here alone with two Karen nurses who had come across from Burma. Doug was the only physician in the district, and the small ten-bed hospital he supervised was usually full. I found him in the hospital and he told me about the great mix of language groups in the area. Ethnic Thai were actually a minority. The majority of the local population were Karens and Mons, who came from Burma. They each have their own languages, but may use Burmese when communicating with each other.

The Thai Government district office was located at the little settlement of Sangklaburi, just across the river. After breakfast we crossed the river in a small boat, and walked over to the District Office with Doug to pay our respects to the government officials. The *Nai Amphur* (District Officer) was there.

"Good morning, sir. How are you this morning?" Doug asked.

"Fine, fine. I see you have some guests."

"Yes. I'd like you to meet Mr. Carder and Mr. Nelson. They have come up from Bangkok for a visit."

"Welcome to Sangklaburi. I think you will find it very quiet here."

"Quiet" is often a Thai euphemism for dull. Such a remote outpost as Sangklaburi would be considered dull by Thai government officials. It is not an honor to be posted in such a distant place. Such positions are usually reserved for young officials just starting on a civil service career, or older officials who have proved to be either incompetent or too competent. Long standing "arrangements" with local hoodlums or corrupt businessmen may be disturbed by an honest and conscientious official.

"I like a quiet place," replied Cecil. "It's too busy in Bangkok."

"I prefer a large city," replied the Nai Amphur, with an unbelieving look.

"Anyway, my family can't live here with me."

Actually, his family could live there too, but many women from the cities refuse to accompany their husbands to remote places. Often this is a joint decision because of their children's education. Parents of educated or middle class backgrounds begin to plan their children's education from the time they start kindergarten. It's important to get into the right school. Some little, one room village school is not the way to begin. Some of the prestigious, secondary schools in Bangkok do provide a better education and a much greater chance of getting into a university. Competition is keen to get into the good secondary schools, which means the student must come from a good elementary school. Because of this system, many government officials serve out their time before retirement in lonely stations, such as Sangklaburi, without their families. Some of these men may resort to whiskey or other women. Some make frequent trips to be with their families, neglecting their official duties. Most accept the situation as their *karma* (fate) and carry on. The Nai Amphur chatted with us in a friendly manner. Being the only doctor in this area Doug's presence was much appreciated. Doug told the Nai Amphur of some villages where Government Malaria Control teams should visit to spray the houses with DDT to kill the malaria spreading mosquitoes.

Leaving the Nai Amphur, we crossed over on a high swinging suspension bridge made of bamboo to a Mon village. The Mons were a powerful group in Burma in ancient times, but were defeated by the Burmese. Many moved across into Thailand. Their bamboo houses were well constructed, neat and clean. Mons are strong Buddhists and this village had a Buddhist priest who was noted for his leadership ability. The bridge we had crossed was his idea. Doug had recently started a malaria control program in the village with the cooperation of the priest. We found him near the village temple, and while Doug talked with him, I investigated the temple. It was constructed of wood with a high arching roof shingled with ceramic tile. A gong made from an empty bombshell hung near the front entrance.

Slipping off my shoes, I went inside. It took a while before my eyes adjusted to the dimly lighted interior. A pleasant odor of burning incense permeated the air. I was standing in a large hall, and at the far end was the great golden Buddha image about fifteen feet high sitting on a raised platform. Incense sticks were burning on both sides of the image. Village images like this one are made of plaster covered with gold paint. Some temples in Bangkok and other large cities do have real gold images. Back outside on the front steps I looked down at the Kwai River and one of its tributaries that entered at that point. Small temple bells, hanging from the high roof, were tinkling in the breeze. The noon sun reflected off the swift flowing water below. Mon women dressed in sarongs were washing clothes at the river's edge while their small children played in the water. Yes, it was quiet, but to me it was not dull.

In the afternoon Cecil and I visited the hospital where Doug was operating on a man wounded in a hunting accident. Several buckshot-sized pellets from a muzzleloader had entered his body, and he had lost a lot of blood. He needed a transfusion badly, but his relatives, who had brought him in, refused to give their blood. Villagers often have a superstitious belief that having their blood extracted will cause them to get sick. Visitors to this hospital may be told their blood is needed and lose a pint before they know what is going on. Cecil and I were no exception. Doug tested our blood but it proved to be the wrong type. We later learned the patient survived, but his recovery was delayed because of lack of blood for a transfusion.

The hospital had only ten beds. Eight were occupied. Families of patients living some distance away were camping around the hospital grounds cooking food for their ill family member. As in most small Thai hospitals, meals were not provided by the hospital. Many patients are not brought in until the services of spirit doctors or home remedies have proved ineffectual. By that time the patient is nearly dead and may not recover.

Toward evening Doug took us upstream a short distance by boat to where the "Death Railroad" had crossed over this tributary. Pilings of local hardwood could still be seen in swampy areas along the bank. I could imagine the prisoners working up to their necks in the mud and slimy water. Old bomb craters, half filled with water, were evidence of aerial bombardment from Allied planes as World War II drew to a close. The Corprons and Dodges had salvaged many railroad ties and bridge trestles to use around the mission station.

Mrs. Corpron had modified her cooking practices to the local conditions. For dinner we had jungle fern and banana blossoms for vegetables, and black glutinous rice steamed in green bamboo tubes. We also had white rice and curry, which is standard fare throughout all of Thailand.

I learned many things on that trip and part of my education came from Olive Pa and Olive Mo. They were an elderly Karen couple from Burma who had settled here and were serving as hostel parents at a student hostel built on the mission station for school age children. This hostel enabled children from distant villages to have a place to live while attending the government school at Sangklaburi. Karen people are given a name when they are born, but when they later have children of their own, they are also known by their oldest child's name. *Pa* means father in the Karen language, and *Mo* means mother. The name of this couple's oldest child was Olive, so they became known as Olive Mo and Olive Pa, mother and father of Olive.

Olive Pa and Olive Mo came over to the Corpron house and we visited late into the night. One of the lessons I learned that night was never to underestimate people from remote places, even the most backwoods jungle areas of Thailand. Olive Pa and Olive Mo spoke perfect English with a proper British accent. They were both college graduates from Burma during the English colonial period, and Olive Pa had once traveled to London where he had addressed the English Parliament. In Burma the Karen people were sometimes cruelly oppressed by the Burmese, so during the more that one hundred years of English occupation the Karens were friendly with the English and welcomed their presence. During World War II the English promised the Karens a sort of autonomous Free State within Burma. However, by the time Burma gained her freedom there had been a change of government in England and that promise had been forgotten. Olive Pa was sent by the newly emerging Karen nationalist movement to argue their cause in England, but to no avail. Burma gained her freedom as a unified country, but some of the old suspicions and hatreds between ethnic groups remained.

Many Karens decided to go ahead with the formation of a Karen State, and the Burmese resisted, resulting in warfare, which continues to the present day. Olive Pa and Olive Mo were identified with the Karen Free State movement, so they fled Burma for Thailand. In the United States I had studied about the "primitive" tribal people of Southeast Asia. I had a lot to learn.

For breakfast the following morning we had steamed black glutinous rice as a cereal with brown palm sugar and fresh grated coconut sprinkled on top. Delicious! A young Mon man who worked at the hospital came by and offered to take me on a hike. Doug had suggested to him that I might like to see more of the countryside. First, we went part way up the trail toward Three Pagodas Pass, which is the trail to Burma, and Three Pagodas Pass is near the border. It was about ten miles to the border, so we didn't go that far. We turned off to the west and came to one of the tributaries of the Kwai. There was a boat on the far bank, so my guide swam across and came back for me in the boat. Here we left any semblance of a trail and proceeded through tall jungle.

We came to a clearing covered with grass and vines. In the center of the clearing was an ancient temple site. Nothing was left but a pile of bricks and rubble and a statue of Buddha about eight feet tall. Tangled vegetation covered the whole area. We removed the vines covering the Buddha image, and it proved to be of a style quite different from any I had ever seen. Later Doug told me he had heard about that place, although he had never been there. It was called the temple of the Three Corpses, but Doug did not know the origin of that name.

Upon our return, we came across the Corpron children on an insect collecting excursion. I had noted the results of previous such expeditions cached in jars around the house. A pet gibbon and a small parrot also shared their home. The Corprons have five children. The oldest was at a boarding school in Chiang Mai, Thailand. Mrs. Corpron taught two at home, and two were pre-school. Their life reminded me of the Swiss Family Robinson. There was a lot of wildlife in the area, including two kinds of deer, wild pigs, tigers, leopards, guar (wild cattle), tapir and wild chickens. Wild elephants are to be found some distance away. Doug had also discovered a kind of fish in the river that strikes dry flies. That fish was seldom caught, and the local people were amazed to see him catch them on a fly rod.

Early the next morning Cecil and I left on a local passenger boat going downstream. Shortly after departing, we turned a bend and surprised a group of about ten monkeys playing along the bank. Many of the trees hanging over the river were covered with wild orchids. We went all the way to Kanchanaburi by boat, getting there at 8:00 P.M., traveling after dark again. There we hired a taxi and went on to Bangkok. The rapid transition from Sangklaburi to the rush and noise of metropolitan Bangkok was almost too much. I resolved to finish language study as soon as possible, and find a "quiet" place upcountry to commence our own work.

Our family in Bangkok
August, 1964

TO THE WORK

Toward the end of our period of Thai language study, Cecil Carder came by the house one afternoon.

"Boy, are you lucky!" he said enviously.

"Why is that?" I replied.

"You have been assigned to the best place in Thailand."

"Where's that?"

"Why, Chiang Rai, of course."

Cecil and his family had lived in Chiang Rai before coming to Bangkok and they had enjoyed their stay there. Now we learned that Karen people in the Chiang Rai area had requested us to come and work with them, myself as an agricultural advisor and Dee to work as a visiting home economist in villages.

Cecil continued, "There is a house available already. You can move in anytime."

"What sort of house?" Dee wanted to know.

"Oh you'll love it. We lived in it for several years."

"How many rooms?" Dee wanted details.

"It's a big two story house. You'll love it."

"Is that the only house available?" I asked.

"Well, this one is right in front of Chiang Rai Wityakhom School and my friend Acharn Tongdee, the headmaster, would like Dee to teach an English course to high school students.

So that was it. Well, never mind. The house sounded suitable and I could hardly wait to get out of Bangkok. Chiang Rai's location in extreme northern Thailand, near Burma and Laos, would put us in a cooler climate and far from the polluted canals and noisy streets of Bangkok.

Still, Bangkok did have its charms. As our time there drew to a close, we kept making "one more trip" to the weekend market at the Pramane Ground near the Royal Palace to view the rich variety of goods for sale and to see the kites flying over the Temple Of The Emerald Buddha. Kites and temple roofs will always be in my mind's eye when I think of Bangkok. "One more trip" to the Bangrak Market on New Road to purchase sticky rice and mango dessert from the betal nut chewing Thai woman, and Chinese roast duck from the Cantonese man who sold ducks and barbecued red glazed pork.

We packed up all of our belongings in crates and steel barrels and sent them off with a transport company to be trucked to Chiang Rai. On the day of our departure Cecil picked us up in his car to take us to Hua Lampong, the central Bangkok train station. Gee and Aroon said their respectful goodbye to us and tears filled their eyes as they held Rebecca and Lani for the last time. They had practically raised Rebecca for the 18 months of our residence in Bangkok. We would miss them.

We boarded the Northern Express to Chiang Mai and pulled out of the station at 5:00 P.M. It was hot at first, but soon the evening coolness flowed in the open windows as we passed through the flat rice fields of central Thailand. It was nearly dark when we passed Ayutthaya, the old capitol city of Thailand, sacked and destroyed by a Burmese army 200 years previously. The old city was gone, but the spires of decaying temples still reached heavenward. The ancient temples, located near a great bend in the Chao Phraya River, extend over an area of several miles, giving an indication of the great city that once thrived in that place.

We were in a second class sleeper car, and shortly after dark a steward came through making up the sleepers. Lani was fascinated by the process in which our seats were converted into double bunk beds, and delighted by her vantage point in an upper berth where she could peek through the curtains. I enjoy rail travel and the Northern Express didn't let me down. I slept soundly through the night, lulled by the gentle rocking of the train. In the morning we woke in the green forested mountains of the north, and pulled into the Chiang Mai station at 8:00 A.M., the end of the rail line.

We stayed in Chiang Mai for a few days, buying supplies and getting acquainted with the battered old Land Rover that had been assigned to us. It steered hard, bounced and rattled like an old wagon without springs, but the engine was sound. It was a pickup type Land Rover with a canvas top over the back. A winch was mounted on the front bumper and it had two spare tires; one mounted behind the cab and one lying flat on the hood.

Into that faded green vehicle we placed a conglomeration of suitcases, boxes, and miscellaneous supplies purchased in Chiang Mai, a larger city than our destination. Early one morning we pulled out of town heading for Chiang Rai. Although Chiang Rai was north we had to go south for about two hours to get on the main road to Chiang Rai. There was no direct road.

The four of us sat in the cab. Lani was five years old and Rebecca 18 months. Between gear shifts on the floor, water bottles, lunch basket and dolls, there was not a lot of room. Yet, on moving day we wanted to be together to face the future as a family.

I often think of my life as divided into definite periods of time: the young days on the farm, the time in the Army, college, Montana and Bangkok. I realized as we drove along on the rain soaked muddy roads that July day in 1965 that I was entering a new segment of my life. Transitions are not always easy as the old and familiar passes and the new and unfamiliar looms ahead. Chiang Rai definitely loomed ahead. What would I do there? Would the people accept me? Would they be able to understand my Bangkok Thai? This was no ordinary transition. Even the move from Montana to Bangkok seemed easy by comparison. No responsibilities awaited us in Bangkok, except learning a language. In Bangkok older and experienced friends were present to advise. In Chiang Rai we would be alone. All I knew was that I was supposed to open an agricultural development program among the Karen and Lahu tribal people. Also, just before leaving Bangkok, I had been informed that I should give some supervision to an elementary school started by the Mission in the Karen village of Namlat, near Chiang Rai.

The uncertainties of an unknown future were dispelled somewhat by the beauty around us. The rainy season was well along and it was rice transplanting time. Groups of farmers, consisting of men women and children, were busy at work stooping in the flooded paddy fields sticking the foot long rice shoots in the mud. It was a time of gaiety in spite of the hard work. We received many a cheery wave as we drove along.

Mountains were visible on all sides, covered with green vegetation. Most of the time the road followed low lying valleys, crossing a mountain pass only to enter another valley. Only a small portion of the road was hard surface. Much of it necessitated grinding along in second gear. After about four hours we arrived in Lampang, which was only as far north as Chiang Mai. We had completed our swing to the south and north again. We stopped to eat a picnic lunch in the shade of teak trees alongside a temple in a village just beyond Lampang. I was eager to get to Chiang Rai before dark, so kept on driving, stopping only to eat and buy gas. It was a long and tiring day. The children were restless. Lani kept asking if we were in Chiang Rai yet. Occasional rain showers forced us to shut the windows, trapping the steamy heat in the car.

Finally, ahead of us, squatting on the flat rice paddies and ringed by mountains, appeared the provincial capitol of Chiang Rai. It was a welcome sight. Huge spreading rain trees covered the quiet outlying streets. Rice mills hummed as the product of thousands of small farms was milled, polished and bagged. Main Street was composed of two-story wooden shops, their Chinese owners selling goods on the ground level and living above.

The house we were to live in was a large old building painted blue. It was surrounded on two sides by Chiang Rai Wityakhom School. An elderly Thai man came out of the house to meet us. He turned out to be Loong In, the gardener- watchman. Loong In was relieved to see us because our belongings from Bangkok had preceded us, and he had been fearful of robbers.

Our trip had taken more than eleven hours over bone-shaking roads in a seemingly springless vehicle. We were exhausted. What we should have done was checked into a hotel and eaten in a restaurant. Still inexperienced, and wary of upcountry hotels and eating places, we immediately began to open the crates and barrels in which our belongings were packed. I found a camp stove and set it up for Dee.

"Oh good, you found a stove. Does it work?"

"I'll have to buy some gas first. Do you need anything else?"

"Bring back something to cook on it."

I bought some gas for the stove at a gasoline station and went on to the open market. The food stalls were all closed.

"Why is the market closed?" I asked a passerby.

"Oh, it's too late," he replied. "They close before dark."

"Where can I buy something to eat?"

"Over there," replied the man, pointing down main street.

I walked down the street looking in each shop until I came to a dimly lit building that offered some possibilities.

"Do you have any food here?" I asked the proprietor.

"Try the restaurant across the street," he replied.

"No, I mean like canned food to take home to eat."

"Oh yes, we have, we have. What would like?"

I looked around the small shop and saw boxes of crackers, jars of candy and cans of cooking oil. Our previous conversation had been in Thai, but he surprised me by switching to English.

"How about a can of Vienna Sausages?" He held up a can for my inspection.

I hadn't dreamed of finding canned Vienna Sausages in Chiang Rai. This place was full of surprises.

"That would be fine. Now, what can I eat with them?"

"May I suggest some bread?" He came up with a loaf of sliced white bread from behind a counter.

"Great, I'll take it too," and made my departure.

That was my first visit to Sipio Store. There were to be many more. When I arrived back at our house Dee was still unpacking.

"Look what I bought, Vienna Sausages and white bread. Let's eat."

"What did that can of sausages cost?"

"Never mind, there was nothing else in town at this hour."

We placed newspapers on an old table and sitting on boxes enjoyed our first meal in Chiang Rai.

We didn't have any bed frames, only mattresses, so we laid those on the floor. Lani and Rebecca immediately fell asleep, so Dee and I took a better look at our new home. It had two floors with large rooms and high ceilings. A single, dim light bulb dangled down from the ceiling in each room. We decided that we would live in the upper story only. That floor provided us with two bedrooms, two bathrooms, kitchen, dining room, living room and a smaller room that was to become Lani's classroom when Dee taught her through a correspondence course. Downstairs was a large room with a fireplace at one end, another room with a fireplace, which I claimed as an office, a bedroom, laundry room and storeroom. Those decisions made, we also retired to our mattress and spent our first night in Chiang Rai.

We were awakened the next morning by a blast of Western marching music.

"What in the world is that," Dee exclaimed, jumping up.

"I can't imagine."

We hurried to the window of a screened porch overlooking the school from which the music seemed to be coming. There was no band, but we soon realized the music was a recording overly amplified through a loud speaker mounted in front of the yellow brick school building. Already students were arriving, boys dressed in white shirts and blue shorts and girls in white blouses and blue skirts. Each student had the abbreviation of the school and his or her student number embroidered on their shirt or blouse. A teacher appeared, blew a whistle, and the students formed into ranks in front of the school. As the Thai flag was raised the children sang the Thai National Anthem and dispersed to their classrooms. A new day had begun in Chiang Rai.

Our first house in Chiang Rai was an old Presbyterian Mission house.

(Lani and Rebecca playing in the yard of our first Chiang Rai house.

We lived in Chiang Rai for nearly seven years and came to love it. It was a friendly community with a great variety of people. The storekeepers and businessmen were of Chinese origin, mostly Taechu and Hakka with a sprinkling of Cantonese. There were also some immigrants from the Indian sub-continent, both Hindus and Muslims. The bulk of the population, including the government officials and school teachers, were Thai. The local Thai, known as *Khon Muang* (people of the land) spoke the Northern Thai dialect, which sounded odd to our "Bangkok ears." We found they could understand us, however, and we in turn learned the northern accent and some new vocabulary.

As the "resident foreigners" in town we were invited to many social functions. When the governor of the province and his wife celebrated their 25th wedding anniversary we were invited. We were invited to new store openings, weddings and funerals. I became a charter member when a Rotary Club was organized. Membership was restricted to men, but there were frequent social gatherings in which wives and children were invited. Through Rotary we got to know many of the business and professional people.

Hawaii Night at a Rotary Club party. Dee received a prize from the Deputy Governor of Chiang Rai Province for most authentic costume.

I became known as the one to go to for assistance when local officials had to deal with foreigners. One day a municipal worker came to my house with a request.

"*Acharn* (teacher), please come with me quickly."

"What's wrong," I asked.

"Some *Farangs* (foreigners) are taking pictures in the fresh market."

"What's wrong with that?"

"They are only taking pictures of garbage and dirty places. Come with me, I can't speak any foreign languages."

I went with him to the market, and there was a European film crew taking movies of the worst parts of the market. The city official said Thailand would be shamed if those movies were shown in foreign lands. I talked to the film crew and explained to them the concerns of the city official. "Too bad, we're just leaving anyway. Tell your friend we also filmed good things." They hopped in their van and left. I really hadn't done anything, but the man from the Chiang Rai City Municipality thought I was responsible for chasing them away. "You live here, so you understand us," he said gratefully. "There are many beautiful places around here where they could do their photography."

On Sunday mornings we usually walked, or took a boat on the Mae Kok River, to the Karen church at Namlat Village. In town there were both Thai and Chinese churches that we occasionally visited.

Dee started teaching English at Chiang Rai Wityakhome School, and we were drawn into the social life of that institution. I found the school at Namlat Village, known as Sahasatsuksa School, bursting at the seams. A number of Lahu people from Burma, fleeing political unrest in that country, had come into Chiang Rai province and wanted to send their children to school. They felt more at home in that school, where most of the students were Karen, a tribal people like themselves.

Khru Arom, headmaster at the school, was glad to get some help in making decisions about the influx of new students. There was no room for all the children who wanted to attend the school, so decisions had to be made about who to accept, who to turn down, whether or not to build more classrooms and dormitories, and where to get the money if we did want to build. I experienced no problems of acceptance there, and ventured out to some villages, Karen and Lahu.

"*Thra (*teacher*)*, where have you been? We've been waiting for you."

"Well, I had to study Thai first."

"Yes, but now you're here and I want to show you a piece of land I've cleared. What should I plant on it that would be good to sell? I want your advice."

Apparently Cecil had mentioned something to them about the new agricultural advisor that was coming.

"Spend the night in my house," many people in the villages asked me. "I have many questions to ask you."

Why had I worried about what I would do? At last, it was time to get to work.

AN ADVOCATE

One day, not long after we had moved to Chiang Rai, some Karens from a nearby village came to visit me. They needed an advocate.

"*Thra* (teacher), can you help us? One of our people is in the police station accused of theft. They are beating him."

"What has he done?" I inquired.

"Nothing at all. He is a good man and would never steal anything. The police won't listen to us."

They explained to me that this man was working for a town family as a gardener. Some jewelry was missing from the house and another Thai servant had accused the Karen man. The police took the Karen to the police station and were beating him to extract a confession.

"*Thra*, you must go and talk to the police. They will listen to a *Farang*."

I really did not want to go. I still felt like a newcomer to this country. I was concerned that my Thai language ability would not be adequate. Most of all, I hated to get involved with the police. Still, this man's friends had already been to the police station and could do nothing. I was their last hope.

"Yes, I will go." I reluctantly replied. "When is a good time?"

"Now, *Thra*, now! They are beating him."

I went to the police station and inquired about the man accused of robbery. They showed me where he was sitting at one end of the old wooden station. His face was badly swollen from beatings.

"Who is in charge of this man's interrogation?" I asked.

"I am," replied a police officer. "We think he is a thief."

"Maybe it would be best if you didn't beat him." I said. "Is that allowed in Thailand?"

"Oh never mind," continued the officer. "He is only a Karen."

My heart sank. It was like hearing an American police officer use a racial slur. I felt sorry for the man, and ashamed for the police officer who should have known better. I looked at the seated Karen with the swollen face who had just heard himself described as "only a Karen."

"Let's go." I said to the man and took him by the hand. We walked out and I took him home. Several days later it was found that the Thai servant had been the thief. I had been a reluctant helper, but it was not to be the last time I was called upon to be an advocate for someone who was discriminated against. My education into the social structure of Thailand had begun.

CULTURAL DIVERSITY

Dee and I knew that Chiang Rai Province had a large population of ethnic minorities, known as the Mountain Tribes. We began to see them in the markets as they came out of the hills to sell forest products and dried chili peppers. They would purchase necessities, such as machetes, ax heads, salt and cloth. We soon learned to recognize each group by their distinctive tribal dress. Six of those tribal groups lived in Chiang Rai Province and other northern provinces.

The Karens were the largest group numerically, with about 200,000 in Thailand and many more in Burma. They had also been in Thailand the longest, at least 200 years. The Karens preferred the lower valleys in the hills and made irrigated rice fields if possible. They usually had to supplement those with hill fields cut out of the hillside forests. Karen women were excellent weavers on backstrap looms and made their own homespun cotton garments of long red skirts and pullover blouses trimmed in yellow, black or blue. Dee inquired about the colors and received different answers. Sometime they would say, "Red and yellow are for flowers, blue is the sky and black is the earth." The men wore a red pullover shirt made by their wives or mothers. Usually, they wore trousers, like the Northern Thai, purchased in the markets. Men from more traditional villages wore long shirts, like a gown, and no pants. Unmarried girls and women wore a long white shift. White was for purity. All the women wore necklaces of seed beads.

The Karens were a very frugal people, preferring to purchase land or livestock rather than consumer goods. They did not like conflict and would go to great lengths to avoid arguments. Sometimes, if there was a land or irrigation water conflict with neighboring Northern Thai, they would just leave that place and move farther back into the hills, even if that resulted in an economic loss. Karens were the primary group we were to work with, so needed to learn their language.

Karen women from Pa Pae Kee.

There were also many Lahu people in Chiang Rai Province. Lahus also lived in Burma, Laos and Southwest China. Some of the Red Lahu subgroup had lived in Chiang Rai Province for many years. Many more Yellow Lahu moved into Thailand from Burma about the time we arrived in Chiang Rai. They were fleeing civil unrest in Burma. The Lahu had no irrigated rice fields, so depended entirely on slash-burn shifting cultivation.

To the dismay of Thai government authorities they cut and burned large areas of forest to plant rice, corn and chili peppers. The corn and dried chilies were sold as cash crops.

The Lahu were more willing than Karens to spend their money. Radios with short wave bands were a favorite. Some of the Lahu subgroups also planted the opium poppy as a cash crop. Dress depended on their subgroup, but the women liked to wear silver necklaces, earrings and bracelets. Lahu men were great hunters. I usually ate wild game meat when visiting their villages, such as deer, wild pig, monkeys, and large lizards. Once, I ate the meat of a guar, the wild cattle of South and Southeast Asia. I ate all kinds, but monkey meat was not my favorite!

Lahu man with his grandson.

A Lahu woman weaving cloth with a backstrap loom.

Some Akha had also lived in Chiang Rai Province for many years, but more were coming in from Burma. There were also Akha in Northern Laos and Southwest China. Akha women used a simple frame loom to weave their blue, almost black, garments which they dyed with indigo, and edged with colorful embroidery. Women wore a short, pleated skirt with a jacket top and a distinctive headdress with a lot of silver and bits of dyed monkey fur on it. They also wore colorful leggings. Because of their black clothes, Thai people sometimes referred to them as "the mountain crows." Akha considered that to be a pejorative.

Akha woman and children.   Akha woman in her house

Akha married couple.

Hmong, locally called Meo, had been moving southward from China for many generations. In Thailand they usually occupied the highest mountain ranges. They planted hill rice, corn and opium poppies. They also planted a native peach which produced small fruit suitable for pickling. Both men and women wore silver jewelry. White Hmong women wore trousers and Blue Hmong women wore a pleated skirt with a batik design. Their skirts were often woven from marijuana hemp fiber. Surely, White and Blue Hmong were one ethnic group many years ago, but must have been separated geographically. Now, their language and dress is different.

Blue Hmong young women.

The Lisu were also known for planting opium in their highland fields. Lisu women wore bright outfits of blue, green and red with a black turban adorned with tassels. Tassels were also attached to the back of their tunics by a sash. I seldom went to Hmong or Lisu villages, but often saw them in the markets.

Two Lisu young ladies.

Mien, called Yao by some, usually lived at high elevations, but some were in low valleys and made irrigated rice paddies. The Mien also had origins in China and had been influenced by Chinese culture. Many could speak Chinese (Yunnanese dialect) and some of the men were even literate in Chinese. Mien women wore ornately embroidered pants and a red muff around the front of their blouses. Only Mien and Hmong houses were built on the ground, likely because their origins were to the north in China. The other tribal groups built their houses elevated off the ground.

The women of all these groups adorned themselves with their distinctive tribal dress and jewelry. Why? I could only guess. To make a statement perhaps of who they were. They were proud of their ethnicity and of their oral history.

Those were the people we encountered in northern Thailand. They mostly lived in the remote hill areas keeping to their own traditions. Nearly all of them practiced slash-burn shifting cultivation on the mountain slopes. To make a hill field, trees would be cut and allowed to dry during the dry season. Burning was usually done in March, before the rains began. Sometimes we would see the hillsides on fire at night. If we were close enough we could hear the roar of the fire going up a hillside and the popping of bamboo sections as they exploded from the hot air trapped inside. At that time the atmosphere all over northern Thailand would be smoky. Large pieces of ash, probably from bamboo, would float down into the town of Chiang Rai.

Hill rice, a dryland variety, would be planted when the rainy season began in April or May. The rice would grow through the rainy season and be harvested in September or October. No cultivation was used; just cutting and burning. A dibble stick (pointed stick) was used to punch a hole in the ground and seeds planted in the holes. Some hand weeding would be done while the rice was growing. Usually, a field was used only one or two years before being allowed to go back to trees and brush. After a fallow period of five to six years the land could be cleared and used again. The mountain people claimed their rice was better tasting and more nutritious than the irrigated rice grown by the lowland Thai. I think that is true. It was delicious.

Lahu man and wife planting rice in a hill field.

Like minority groups in many countries, the Tribal people suffered some discrimination from the majority Thai. Physical characteristics were very similar, so Those who received an education and spoke Thai fluently could meld into Thai society if they wished. However, most Tribal people lived in traditional villages and were often characterized as dirty, having no culture and detrimental to the nation because of forest cutting and opium planting. The police officer, who beat the Karen to extract a confession, was probably from central Thailand and reflected a social discrimination unfortunately found in many areas of the world.

LEARN FROM THE PEOPLE

When we started our work among the tribal people in the 1960's Mao Zetung ruled supreme in China. Thailand did not border China, but Northern Thailand was not far from the China border. The Thai government was anti-Communist and many people were fearful of their country being infiltrated by Thai and Laotian dissidents who had received training in China. Radio Beijing had a Thai language radio broadcast every night at 10:00 P.M. and Dee and I often listened to it on the shortwave band of our radio. Poor rural Thai and the ethnic minorities were obviously the targets of those broadcasts. The Chinese Communist system was praised, The United States was condemned and the Thai government denounced as "the running dogs of the imperialists."

We knew that many other people, including some of the people we were working with, also listened to those broadcasts. We resolved that we would not be "Ugly Americans," but try to live a plain lifestyle, spend time with the people and help them as best we could.

One of Mao Zetung's dictums was "Learn From The People." I was certainly no disciple of Mao, but I realized that I did need to learn from the people. Although I was born and raised on a Midwestern farm, had a Masters Degree in Agriculture and had worked for the Agricultural Extension Service in Montana,

I was now confronted by some very different agricultural systems, different kinds of crops, different weather and people of a different culture whose world view was very different from mine. I had a lot to learn.

We did a one month crash course in the Northern Thai dialect, but soon turned our attention to learning the Karen language. We hired a young man, named Shwe Po, to come to our house every morning. He was not a trained teacher, but did some gardening and found some occasional work around town. He was an intelligent man and could speak, read and write both Karen and Thai very well. We had some language lessons written in both English and Karen. Po Shwe could not read or speak English, so we had to communicate in the Thai language. It was rather awkward, and our progress was slower than it had been in the Thai language school, which had very good teachers. Karen is a totally different language; not related to Thai in any way. It sounds beautiful when spoken by a native speaker. It is a tonal language and every syllable ends in a vowel, which makes it sound rather poetic. The written language uses the Burmese alphabet, which at first looked to us like nothing but a series of circles.

One of the first phrases we learned was how to greet people: *ner o chu ah,* which means, "Are you well?" Unfortunately, I learned it wrong and went around greeting people by saying, *"ner chu o ah?"* which means "Do you have any hair?" When I finally got that straightened out I realized why people grinned every time I used those words!

Dee and I studied the Karen language together, but she also had another major task. Lani was now of kindergarten age, so Dee taught her each afternoon with the help of Calvert Correspondence Course sent from the United States. In the morning Lani attended the Thai school next door for two years and studied her correspondence lessons in the afternoon.

I began to spend some time in both Karen and Lahu villages. At first I carried too much "stuff" with me. Someone usually volunteered to carry my heavy backpack over the foot trails, but I soon learned to travel light. I quit using a backpack and just rolled up a change of clothe, towel and blanket in a loin cloth and slung it over my back as the local people did. The loin cloth could be used like a bathing suit when bathing in a stream or river. I bought a straw hat in the market and often used the rubber sandals, known in English as flip-flops. The village people were very hospitable and I would always be invited to sleep in a house and eat with the family. I ate what was put in front of me and found it to be nourishing, if not always to my taste. Over time, the food even became delicious. It was always rice, usually with some curry, boiled vegetable and chili paste. It was impossible for a foreigner to totally blend in, but I tried.

In a Lahu house. Chili peppers drying on rack above fire.

An opportunity soon presented itself to be of some real use. I had helped the Karen village of Mae Yao order some fruit trees from a government nursery. I hadn't thought about how the trees would be delivered. In fact, they weren't delivered. I was told that they had arrived at the government agricultural office and I should pick them up. They were lychee trees, which has a delicious fruit and sells for a good price. Villagers could plant a few trees around their houses and the fruit would be a good source of income.

Someone suggested that the new agricultural missionary should be responsible for getting the trees to their destination, so I picked up the trees at the agricultural office and loaded them in our Land Rover pickup. They were marcotted trees, which are obtained by cutting off the bark in a circle around a small branch on a living tree, wrapping that place with coconut husk and covering the husk with plastic. When kept moist, roots will appear and grow into the husk. The branch can then be cut off and planted. The trees were not potted, so were not too heavy. However, they needed to be sent to their destination. It was the beginning of the monsoon season when trees should be planted so their roots will get established before the dry season. There were no telephones and the road to Mae Yao village was impassable to vehicles because of the rains.

I transported the trees to the nearby Karen village of Namlat and recruited Po Swe, our Karen language teacher, to help me carry the trees to Mae Yao Village located at the end of a muddy twelve kilometer road overflowing with swollen streams. We placed 20 trees in a large basket made from split bamboo, put a bamboo pole through the handles and, carrying the weight on our shoulders, started walking.

The heavy load and the hot humid weather soon caused me to perspire heavily. My American shoulder was unused to a carrying pole and began to hurt. To "learn from the people," had a certain idealistic appeal. An appeal, I noted, that was dissipating as fast as my bodily fluids. "This is not the way to do it," I complained. "The people who ordered these trees should carry them."

My comrade at the other end of the carrying pole was more accustomed to such burdens. He did not complain. He even whistled a tune from time to time. About half way to our destination he quoted a verse from the Bible. I assumed it was aimed at me. He spoke in Thai. Perhaps it was his own free translation, but what he said was very clear. "He who would a leader be, must first be a servant." I contemplated his words as we trudged on. My friend taught me a good lesson that day. I had to learn many more, but that was a beginning.

We did get the trees to Mae Yao village. They were planted and grew into big trees which produced an abundance of lychee fruit every April. Over the years, whenever I returned to that village I found I had some credibility there. Relationships were made with those people that still exist. They didn't forget who had carried in their fruit trees in a basket on a carrying pole. Learn from the people.

VISA TRIPS

We had entered Thailand on temporary visas with the expectation of obtaining a permanent non-immigrant visa after arriving. The Thai Immigration Department would only give 200 permanent visas each year to citizens of each country that applied for them. In the 1960's many Americans were coming to live and work in Thailand, so there was more competition for the 200 visas granted to Americans. We had to wait.

Our temporary tourist visas were only good for three months. At the end of that time we had to leave the country and re-enter with another three month visa. While living in Bangkok we would fly to Penang, Malaysia for that purpose. Penang is located on the western coast, just south of the Thai border. It was a nice place to visit, but not much fun with two small children. Rebecca was still in diapers and disposable diapers were not available.

Just before leaving Bangkok for Chiang Rai we received a notice to come to the Immigration Office to pick up our visas, but when we arrived only mine was there. Dee's had disappeared. An immigration officer said it should be there and searched for it. Finally, he sheepishly said it could not be found. American companies were willing to pay large sums of money under the table to get visas for their employees assigned to Thailand. Apparently, her visa had been given to someone with deeper pockets.

In Chiang Rai Dee still had to leave the country every three months. We could, however, enter Laos for that purpose. The Mekong River was only a two hour drive east of us over a new road. It was not a hard surface road, but was passable at all seasons. When we crossed the river we were in Laos. Chiang Khong was the border town on the Thai side. We had to officially depart Thailand by getting Dee's passport stamped at the Immigration Office in Chiang Khong, and in that sleepy little border town there was only one immigration official and he did not get much business. We usually had to go looking for him in a coffee shop. He would grudgingly return with us to his office where he stamped Dee's passport

With her passport complete with a departure stamp we drove on to the bank of the Mekong River. The Mekong is a mighty river, originating in the Himalayan Mountains and passing through Southwest China before becoming the border between Thailand and Laos. It was a large river with swift and treacherous currents. During the monsoon season it was swollen with heavy rain and was rather intimidating. There were always boat boys waiting to take passengers across the river in their long-tailed motor boats. These boys appeared to be about 13 or 14 years of age, and had been hired by the boat owners to run the boats. Lani and Rebecca were included on their mother's passport so they had to go with us. I was a little reluctant to place our lives in the hands of those boat boys, so after our first crossing I purchased life vests for us to wear. There were often too many people in the boat, so it rode low in the water. It only took about 10 minutes to cross the river, but someone usually had to bail out water that leaked in. Fortunately, we made three or four crossings a year without any bad experience.

Boats on the Mae Khong River.

On the Lao side we docked at the town of Ban Huey Sai, a very interesting place, where it was best not to ask people what they did for a living. It was during the time of the CIA funded war against Laotian and Vietnamese Communists. Some *Farang* men could always be seen on the streets. Some were pilots who flew unmarked airplanes on bombing raids against the Communists, or supported the Hmong guerrilla forces recruited by the CIA. Ban Huey Sai was also an opium marketing center, and a market town for many Hill Tribe people from the surrounding mountains. There was a Tom Dooley hospital, which added to the ethnic mix. Tom Dooley was an American medical doctor who started some hospitals in remote areas of Laos. He recruited doctors and nurses from several different countries. On a hill above the town was an old French fort, dating back to the French colonial period. It reminded me of old movies about the French Foreign Legion.

After arriving in Ban Huey Sai we climbed up to the Lao police station on a hill to get Dee's passport stamped before noon. Laotian civil servants enjoyed a siesta from noon to 3:00 P.M. There seems to be an inverse relationship between the size of a country and the size of its visa stamp in your passport. Laos had a big stamp.

After our official business was completed we always returned to the market area to look in the shops which sold antiques and Hill Tribe artifacts. Some stores also sold imported canned fruit, which was duty free, and also products from China that were not available in Thailand. Soon it was time to cross the river again, find the Thai Immigration official and get Dee stamped back into Thailand as a new resident again for three months.

We were later told by the principal of Chiang Rai Witayakhome School that the Immigration official on the Thai side had a daughter at Witayakhome School who was in Dee's English class. On our next trip we mentioned that to the official and afterwards received fast and efficient service from him.

Those large Laos immigration stamps filled Dee's passport rather rapidly. We had to go to the American Embassy in Bangkok and have extra accordion pages added to her passport. Before going on an immigration trip to Laos, Dee had to get a Laotian visa stamped in her passport at the Laotian Embassy in Bangkok. That was also a large stamp. For convenience Dee's passport was kept at our Mission Office in Bangkok and Cecil Carder would take it to the Laotian Embassy when needed to get the visa stamp and mail the passport to us in Chiang Rai. Cecil took it in for a visa stamp one time not realizing the pages were all full. When he came to pick it up the young lady clerk at the Embassy told him of that problem.

"Mr., the pages in that passport were all full when you brought it in."

"Oh, I'm sorry," replied Cecil, "I didn't know that."

"Not to worry," said the clerk, "I just cut a page out of some other American passport and taped it in your book."

Cecil didn't think that was quite legal, but it was already done. It worked fine, until we were back in California during our first furlough. We needed to get new passports, so sent in the old ones and applied for new ones at the U.S. State Department, Passport Division in Los Angeles. I received my new passport, but Dee's was held up. Finally, Dee received a letter from the Passport Division demanding an explanation about the extra page. She was warned that defacing an American passport was a serious matter. Her explanation must have been accepted, as she received a new one just before we needed to return to Thailand. We often wondered what happened to that other American whose passport was missing a page!

As resident aliens we also had to check in at the Chiang Rai Police Station. Our history was written down and we were fingerprinted. Even Lani and Rebecca had to put their small fingers in the ink blotter and put their prints on an official form. Now, forty years later, those prints are probably still on file in some dusty folder in that police station. Eventually, Dee also received her permanent visa and both of us had Alien Registration Books which allowed us to stay indefinitely as long as we renewed them each year at the police station. No more trips across the Mekong. No more glimpses of spooks (intelligence agents) in Ban Huey Sai. I kind of missed those trips!

A ROAD WITH A JINX

Some of the mountain roads I drove on in Thailand must have been about the worst in the world. There were very steep grades, abrupt drop offs on either side, no bridges, stumps in the middle of the road, mud or dust according to the season, and hairpin turns so tight they required backing up and inching forward two or three times to navigate the turn. Village people in the mountains did not have motorized vehicles and could not judge if a road could be used or not. When asked if a certain road was passable they would invariable reply, "Oh yes, no problem." I learned to take such replies with a grain of salt. There were no roads at all to many villages, so a long walk was required to reach them. It was a challenge, however, to try to reach those villages in my 4-wheel drive vehicle, or, at least, to get as close as possible before shouldering a back pack and walking. There were times when I should have stopped driving sooner and started walking earlier.

Winching up an embankment in my Land Rover after fording a river.

One such occasion was going to the Karen village of Mae Hang. There was an oxcart track to that village and the villagers assured me my 4-wheel drive, Land Rover pickup would have no problem. Of course, there was a problem. Oxcarts have about two feet of clearance from axle to ground. There was tall grass growing between the wheel tracks and I was concerned about stumps concealed in the grass. Again the villagers assured me there were no stumps. Fortunately, I was driving slowly, but it was still quite a jolt when I hit the hidden stump of a tropical hardwood. I hit it hard enough to punch a hole in the front differential housing. I could go on, but did not dare engage the front wheel drive for fear of gear oil leaking out and damaging the gears.

I made it to the village anyway, but that night it rained long and hard. That really made me nervous, because I had forded a river coming in and the rain would surely raise the water level. The next day I drove out all the way in only two wheel drive. I had to winch out of a couple of mud holes, after chasing out the water buffaloes that love to wallow in such places. The river was just before the main road, but it was running high. The fording place had a sandy bottom and appeared to be the best location for a crossing. I would have preferred using 4-wheel drive, but there was no choice but to attempt the ford. I didn't feel like camping by the river for several days. Anyway, it might rain some more. I went on across, and about midway water starting seeping in around the bottom of the doors and flooded the floorboard. I had never driven in water that deep before. It was a great relief to reach the opposite bank and pull up on dry land with water streaming out from under the Land Rover. I made it home that day, but had to have the differential housing repaired before using the vehicle again. There was no damage to the gears.

On two separate occasions I had bad luck attempting to drive to the Karen village of Ban Nawk. Village people believe in ghosts and spirits, so they began to kid me about the ghost that apparently hung out along that road and didn't like my Land Rover. I had been to Ban Nawk several times by the foot trail. It went over a mountain and was about a four hour walk. Other than getting tired legs, that was no problem, but I preferred to drive if possible.

On one occasion, after walking into the village, I was taken to the house of a woman I had met on other visits. Someone said she was sick, and as I entered her house I was confronted with a terrible odor. The woman came crawling out from a bedroom, and I could see she had a terrible sore on her cheek. The odor was almost more than I could stand. Her husband wanted to know if I could do anything for his wife.

"*Thra,* can you do anything to help her? He asked in a desperate voice. "She's in great pain."

I knew there was nothing I could do, but I offered to take her back to the hospital in Chiang Rai.

"She can't walk, we would have to carry her," was the reply.

Some of the village men constructed a simple sedan chair of bamboo, and the following day walked back over the mountain with me to the road. It was a difficult trip, both for the woman and the men who carried her. I put her in the front seat of my Land Rover, and with the windows rolled down, drove back to Chiang Rai, where I left her at Overbrook Hospital. The following morning I returned to talk with Dr. Kampol, the head doctor. "I'm sorry," he said, "but there is nothing I can do. She has face cancer, and the cancer has penetrated all the way through her cheek. The flesh is dead. That's why she smells so bad. I have put a bandage on her face and gave her husband some pills to relieve the pain. The cancer is too far advanced to treat."

It was a disappointment, but there was nothing I could do but send them back by bus. From the road she would have to be carried back to her village again. The bus driver, however, wouldn't let her on the bus. "She smells so bad she will disturb the other passengers," he complained. He was right, but I insisted. "She can sit in the rear next to an open window," I argued. Reluctantly, he let her on. A few weeks later I heard she had died.

Woman with face cancer being carried in a sedan chair.

The people in that village had requested a good boar pig to cross with their small native pigs. They had seen the results of such crossings in other villages where I had brought in a boar of a Western breed. The offspring were much larger and faster growing, but still had the native hardiness of their mothers. I discovered I could nearly double the meat supply in a village simply by bringing in a good daddy pig. I had a large duroc jersey boar I was reserving for that village, but the problem was getting it there. The four hour walk over the mountain trying to coax a reluctant pig along did not seem like a viable solution.

Finally, during the dry season of 1967 that village sent word that there was now a road to their village and would I please deliver their pig. A logging company was cutting teak trees in that area and a new logging road had been cut through the hills to bring out the logs. That road did not follow the old foot trail, but came in from a totally different direction. I was always optimistic about new roads, sometimes to my sorrow, but it seemed the best way to get that big pig in there.

I traveled with four Karens to help me in case of problems. We loaded the 250 pound hog into the back of my Land Rover pickup and tied it up right behind the cab. Two of the Karens sat up in the cab with me and two in back with the pig. We found the new road, and it was not too bad. Unfortunately, however, those older Land Rovers had a problem. When you drove through water, and the brake linings got wet, you lost the brakes. At one place along that road I had just forded a small stream and immediately went up a steep hill. Nearing the top of the hill I realized I should have geared down, but I was worried about the brakes so tried to make it to the top without shifting. I didn't quite make it. I tried to gear down, but the engine died when I was in neutral. Back down the hill we went without any brakes. I stayed on the road until about half way down, but went off the embankment where the road curved. Fortunately there was a clump of bamboo just in the right place. The Land Rover abruptly stopped up against the bamboo. It was at about a 60 degree angle with only the front wheels up on the road bed.

The pig was hanging from his tether inside the rear of the Land Rover, so I quickly untied the knots and released him. He slid down to the tailgate. The two Karens that had been sitting there were shook up, but not injured. I tried to start the vehicle, but since it was resting in an almost vertical position the fuel pump couldn't pump up enough gas to keep it running. That was a lonely road. No tow service. No AAA. Just five people who considered themselves very fortunate that we hadn't gone all the way over. If that clump of bamboo had not been there we would likely have suffered injuries or worse.

I asked two of the men with me to walk on to the village, which was still several miles ahead of us. Perhaps they could come back with a lot of men who would be able to pull up the Land Rover from its resting place. As we sat and waited I had time to think. First of all, I reminded myself of how dumb I was not to have shifted to a lower gear before going up the steep grade. Secondly, I thanked God for placing that bamboo clump in a strategic location.

After about one hour the two men came back in a truck owned by the timber company. As they were walking to the village they had come to where some men were piling up teak logs using a truck with a heavy winch. That was just what we needed. The truck driver was willing to pull me out if I was willing to pay him 500 Baht in advance. That was about $25.00, and considered a lot of money. I was in no position to bargain, so agreed to his proposition. Five minutes later I was back up on the road. We tied the pig up again and continued on to the village.

That night we had a meeting in one of the homes to decide on arrangements for keeping the boar in the village. One family was elected to keep the pig. They would be responsible for building a simple shed to house him and feed him well. Their payment for doing this was one piglet, of their choice, from each litter fathered by this boar. Everyone agreed. That was basically the system used in other villages and, in most cases, worked well. The pig food was important. The native pigs can get along on rather poor, low protein food. The Western breeds of pigs, however, require more protein, and that duroc jersey did get into trouble about one year later. Apparently, its caretaker was skimping on the feed, so the boar got to catching chickens when they got in his pen and eating them. I had to make another trip to the village to re-establish the guidelines.

The native mountain pigs.

This pig is a 50% offspring of a Hampshire boar crossed with native sow.

We all made it back home to Chiang Rai the next day, but that was the trip that established the ghost theory. About three years later I again agreed to bring an animal to that village via the same road. Ghosts have long memories. That time I had agreed to deliver a young bull. The villagers had managed to purchase six cows from neighboring Thai people, but they had no bull. I heard there were some bulls available in the larger city of Chiang Mai, so I drove there in my old Land Rover and went bull hunting. I found a suitable young bull owned by a Thai man on the outskirts of Chiang Mai. It was 50% Brahma, 25% Holstein, and 25% Zebu, which is the breed of the native cattle in Thailand. I was not interested in milk production. The village people did not drink milk. They just wanted some nice calves to sell.

This bull was still young, but probably weighed about 600 pounds. Much too big to put in my Land Rover, so I borrowed a larger, truck type Land Rover from Jim Conklin, a missionary friend in Chiang Mai. That was a rather odd vehicle, and the Land Rover Company did not make many of them. They had the same wheel base as the ordinary Land Rover, but were much higher. Jim had named this Land Rover "The Monster," and warned me that it was top heavy and tipped over easily. It also needed a new lug wrench and Jim suggested I buy one before leaving town in case I had a flat tire and needed to change wheels. Ben Dickerson, another Chiang Mai based missionary, needed to go to the auto parts store anyway so he offered to buy the new wrench. When he came back with it I started off in "The Monster" with the bull riding high.

The plan was to deliver the bull to Ban Nawk Village, stay one night and return to Chiang Mai. I had two Karens with me in case of trouble, but I really didn't expect any. It was a rather new vehicle, the tires were good, and, anyway, I had a new lug wrench. We had about four hours of driving on good roads before turning onto the logging road that I remembered all too well. Shortly before reaching the place where I had gone off the road with the boar pig three years before I had a flat tire. Not to worry, I had a good spare and a new lug wrench. I removed the spare tire from its location under the rear of the truck and proceeded to loosen the lug nuts on the flat tire. "Oh no!" I cried. The lug nuts were different on "The Monster" and the wrench did not fit them. There was a monkey wrench in the tool kit, but after scraping off the skin on my knuckles I realized the attempt was futile. I could not remove the flat tire. The three of us sat on the ground looking at "The Monster" with the bull in it trying to decide what to do. At that moment a second tire suddenly went flat with a hiss of air. Incredible! Two flat tires, one when the vehicle was parked, and no usable lug wrench. Only one spare tire anyway. I really didn't believe in ghosts, but that almost made a believer out of me.

One of the Karens with me had an idea. He thought there was a dam under construction not too far distant. A lot of people were working there and maybe they could help. The Karen pointed in the general direction and I went off in search of the dam construction site, leaving the two men to watch "The Monster" and the bull. After about a two hour walk I found the construction site. They had a work shop in which they repaired their equipment and could even patch inner tubes. One of the mechanics was willing to drive me back in a pickup, remove one tire from "The Monster", take it back to his shop and patch it, inflate it and bring it back to "The Monster" and put it on. He did not charge me anything, and he also put on the spare tire. Now we had four good tires, but no spare. Most Thai people do have a generous nature. I appreciated his good work very much and tried to pay him, but he would not accept any payment.

I decided, however, that I had enough of that road. Ghost, or no ghost, I was not going to push my luck, especially with no spare tire. The two Karens with me were from Ban Nawk Village, so I asked them to walk the bull on to their village. I was going back to Chiang Mai. Now, however, a new problem presented itself, how to get the bull out of the truck. It was too high for him to jump out; I was afraid he would break a leg. There were no loading chutes, or even embankments I could back up against to unload him, so I decided to bulldog him; tie his legs together and drop him off the back of the truck to the ground. I thought that would be safer than jumping him off.

I was a farm boy, not a ranch kid. I had never bulldogged an animal that big in my life; certainly not a 600 pound bull, but I wanted out of there. It was already late afternoon and soon it would be dark. I found two pieces of rope, put them between my teeth like I had seen in cowboy movies, moved in on the bull, reached down and grabbed his two legs on the far side and pulled on them at the same time as I leaned against him. Down he went on his side with a crash. I think he was more surprised than I was. I tied his two hind legs together and then the front legs. He managed to kick me once in the shoulder during the struggle and I was black and blue for a month. Now that his legs were tied up, I dragged him to the rear of the truck and dropped him off. The two Karen men were aghast. They had never seen a cow, or bull, treated like that.

The bull landed on his back and just laid there for about one long minute. *"Si li,"* exclaimed the Karens. In their language that means he's dead. Soon he began to roll his eyes and I untied the ropes. He stood up and was apparently undamaged. I handed his lead rope to the open mouthed Karens and told them to walk him home. As for me, I drove back to Chiang Mai alone as fast as I could.

I spent that night with Jim Conklin and his wife, Idalene. Jim asked me about my trip. I told him "The Monster" didn't tip over, but that he had better talk to Ben Dickerson about that lug wrench. That old logging road was not maintained and soon became impassable. I never went that way again. Do you suppose that ghost is still there?

A RING FOR THE BULL

From time to time I would hear reports about the bull at Ban Nawk Village. He was getting big. The cows were all with calf. He was getting bigger. All seemed well, until I began to hear some troubling news. It was reported that he was *du*, which means fierce. One day a villager from Ban Nawk came to see me.

"*Thra* (teacher) the bull you brought us is a very good bull, but he is *du mak* (very fierce)"

"What seems to be the problem?"

"No one dares get near him."

"Why not? Does he chase people?"

"No, not yet, but he lowers his head and rumbles in his chest if anyone gets near."

Large animals, such as cattle and water buffalo, are not confined to fenced pastures in tribal villages, but are simply released during the day time. Usually, they are herded back in the evening and are tied up under a house at night. That system usually worked well, but the bull at Ban Nawk was becoming a problem. He hadn't hurt anyone yet, but something had to be done before he did.

"*Thra*," the man continued, "we are all afraid of him. You will have to do something."

"O.K, I will visit your village soon and see what can be done about this matter."

88

When I was a boy on a South Dakota farm my father would put a large brass ring in our bull's nose. A lead rope could then be snapped on the ring when it was necessary to move him from one place to another. A nose is a sensitive place, so even a fierce bull could easily be led. No bull rings were available in Thailand, so I wrote to my father, who was a retired farmer living in Dell Rapids, South Dakota, explaining my problem. He immediately sent back a small package by airmail containing two bull rings.

Now that I had the rings in hand I began to plan a return trip to Ban Nawk, which forced me to think in more detail of what I had to do, and how to do it. I had never actually put a ring in a bull's nose. I only knew it was a commonly accepted practice in the United States where there are such things as cattle barns, bull pens, and equipment to hold the bull while inserting the ring. The ring is a perfect circle, but by unscrewing two small screws the ring can be opened up. The ends that were screwed together are sharply pointed, so it is possible to punch the ring through the septum of the bull's nose, return the ring to its circular shape and replace the screws. Sounded simple, but I began to wonder what a *du* bull was going to think of that procedure and what he would do to me as I was doing it. I knew it had to be me. The villagers sure weren't going to ring that bull. The more I thought about it, the more I sympathized with the mouse that got the idea to bell the cat.

Jim Conklin, the owner of that big Land Rover we called "The Monster," had grown up on a California farm, so I recruited him to go back to the village with me. He had never ringed a bull either, but he readily consented, so I knew he must have been a good friend. The infamous logging road was no longer passable, so we had to take the four hour walk over the foot trail, arriving at the village in late afternoon. The cattle were still out in the surrounding forest, but near evening someone went out to herd them back to the village. One of the cows had a bell around its neck, so it was easy to find them.

Wow! That bull had really grown. I knew I would never bulldog him again. The village people were obviously frightened of him and kept their distance. I believe that was part of the problem. The bull sensed their fear, and knew he could do anything he wanted. If someone did get too close he would lower his head as if to charge and a rumbling sound would come from deep in his chest. He belonged in a Mexican bull fight ring, not in a peaceful Karen village.

By that time the villagers were all standing around watching. We two foreigners either had to do what we came for, or eat humble pie and go home. We looked around for a sturdy tree and found one with a fork in the trunk at about the height of the bull's head. That looked like a good place to tie him. I asked one of the village men to place some salt on the ground near the base of that tree. The animal was hungry for salt and began to greedily lick it up, which gave Jim and me the opportunity to slip a rope around his neck. We quickly pulled his head up into the crotch of that tree, snubbed him in close and securely tied the rope around the tree.

That was easier than I thought it would be. Still, he had a lot of freedom to move around, so I was still concerned about putting the ring through his nose. I had the ring opened up and ready to go, so with a quick movement I thrust the pointed end through his nose septum, squeezed the ring back into its circular shape and screwed the screws back into the brass ring. He really didn't put up much of a struggle at all. He turned out to be a real pussy cat. That bull just had everybody spooked and took advantage of their fear. Before releasing him I snapped a lead rope on the ring, and after untying him demonstrated to the villagers how easy it now was to lead him around. Mission accomplished. Our audience all gave a relieved laugh, and Jim and I felt like heroes.

We stayed in a house in the village that night. For our evening meal we were fed rice and barking deer. The hunters had been lucky. The village men hunted with muzzle loaders so must be quite close to the game before shooting. Reloading takes some time, so they need to fire accurately the first time. Barking deer are a small species of deer found in Southeast Asia and their meat is very delicious. After eating, several of the village men came over to chat. Our host boiled tea and we sat on the floor drinking tea and talking. The men began to talk about a Thai man in a village near the old logging road that had been my nemesis. One man turned to me.

"*Thra*, remember the road you used to drive on? The one with a ghost that didn't like you?" The men all chuckled.

"Yes, I remember that road all too well."

"Maybe that ghost won't be there anymore."

"Why not?"

"A bad man in that village was shot and killed just two days ago."

"Who shot him?"

"We don't know."

"Why was he shot?"

There was some reluctance to talk about that subject, but one man, seeing my puzzled expression, explained.

"That man had the power to do *katah* and used it for evil purposes. He caused the death of many people. Now he is dead and good riddance." *Katah* is something like witchcraft or supernatural charms.

It was believed by the villagers that some people have the power to hurt or kill an enemy. In some cases the power can be used for good, such as healing a sickness or healing a broken bone. Love potions are also related. It is believed that someone who has this power can cause a small piece of bone or wood to magically enter the heart or stomach of an enemy, or perhaps for a needle to puncture the heart. A variation is for a string to slowly wrap around the heart or intestines of a perceived enemy. That usually results in a slow, lingering death. Supposedly, the man in the Thai village had this power and had used it to kill several people. Not surprisingly, someone had decided to eliminate him from the community. The Karens were not involved, but they seemed to agree it was a good thing he was no longer a threat. Those were some of the men who had been kidding me about the ghost along the logging road. I asked them if it was possible for a *katah* to be made against a Land Rover. They all laughed and urged me to try that road one more time now that man was dead.

Jim and I learned about the power of a *katah* that night. The men told us that some Karens had the power too, but they only used it for good, like healing sickness. There is also an antidote against a bad *katah,* which is another *katah* used to nullify the effects of the first one. It was an all male group and soon they got to talking about love potions, which they said are mostly used by young people, both men and women. They believed there are three kinds of love potions. One is called *graesa* in the Karen language. The purpose of that type is to cause a boy or girl, who has jilted you in love, to suffer, or to cause the offending person to separate from a present lover. To put this in effect you must obtain something personal from the one to be charmed, or cursed, such as a piece of clothing or hair. Take this and put it into the shell of a land snail and put the shell into a dove's nest and float it down a stream. When the one to be charmed hears a dove call the spell will come into affect.

We were told about a second type of love charm that both boys and girls have to watch out for. This is called a *rehgaw,* or a "calling someone to love you" charm. Perhaps in some other house that night girls were sitting around the kitchen fire and an older woman was telling them to beware of that same charm. Anyway, to put that into affect you go to a place where no one can hear you and call the name of the one you want to love you and make a *katah*, which is something like saying a magic incantation. The one you called by name will then be irresistibly drawn to you, and even sleep with you if you so wish. This is probably a good excuse for fellows. If they are criticized for fooling around with a girl they can always reply, "She must have strong *katah* and put a love charm on me." Might work!

The third type of love charm is very severe, and not very nice. It is called a *rehsi*, or "death love" charm, and is performed by boys. If a young man wants to kill a girl because she has rejected his advances, he calls her name and make a *katah*. The girl will come to him, prepare food for him, work in his house and even sleep with him, just like a wife. She is under the spell and does not know what she is doing. When the spell is over the girl will come to her senses and realize what she has done. Pre-marital sex is rare among the Karens and strongly condemned, so she will then be so ashamed she will kill herself.

The men were quick to explain that those were just stories about charms and curses that they had heard about from their parents and grandparents. No one did them anymore. Maybe not. Anyway, who can explain love? What can ease the pain of rejected love? What can explain a long, lingering illness when the heart seems to beat fainter and fainter, or the pain in the abdomen is only relieved by death? Those stories do, at least, offer an explanation for some of the mysteries of life and death.

The next morning Jim and I walked back over the mountain, reclaimed my Land Rover from where I had parked it and drove back to Chiang Mai. We knew of one big male that was now cursed with a ring in his nose!

TREKKING

I soon discovered that most of the tribal villages I wanted to visit were not accessible by road. A few were located near the Maekok River and could be reached by boat, but most required a long walk. I also discovered that more language study was necessary. Much of our work was with the Karen ethnic group and we really needed to learn their language. Po Shwe, our language teacher, continued to come to our house for two hours each morning, and Dee and I both continued our struggle to learn that language. It was a slow process and I was getting a little tired of language study, so I did make occasional village trips to provide some variety.

One day I received a letter from a German friend in Chiang Mai. The writer of the letter, Arno Hoppe, was an agricultural adviser attached to a German Government supported dairy and livestock center. Arno liked to hunt and hike in the mountains and was always looking for excuses to pick up his rifle and get away to the hills. Earlier, Arno and I had talked about taking some cows to the Lahu village of Huey Pu in Mae Suey District to help them get started raising cattle. Arno thought he could obtain the cows free of charge. His letter informed me that His Excellency the German Ambassador to Thailand also wanted to take a trek through the mountains of Northern Thailand. Arno was proposing that I accompany them, and that we combine this trek with taking the cattle to the Lahu village, and then continue on through a remote area to the Mae Kok River, a distance of about seventy kilometers. He thought the Ambassador would find that interesting.

I replied, giving my approval, and in a few days I received a letter from the Ambassador informing me that he and his son and his daughter, Gunthar and Katherine, would be arriving in Chiang Rai by plane and would I please meet them and transport them in my Land Rover to Mae Suey District town where we would start our trek. The plan was to meet Arno and his friend, Hardy Stockman, at Mae Suey. They would come from Chiang Mai by truck with the cattle.

On the given date, July 14, 1969, I met the noon plane from Bangkok at the dusty little Chiang Rai airport. The Ambassador, Dr. Ulrich Scheske, and his two children disembarked, and I took them to our house for lunch. Gunthar was studying at a university in Germany and had come to Thailand to visit his parents during the summer vacation. Like his father, he enjoyed hiking and wanted to see remote and distant areas, rather than the usual tourist spots. Katherine was about sixteen and quite able to hold her own in that active family. After lunch, we loaded our Land Rover with our sleeping bags, extra clothes, and several boxes of gifts which the Ambassador intended to hand out to villagers along the route of our trek.

We drove southwest of Chiang Rai to the little town of Mae Suey and parked at a house outside of town belonging to a Thai farm family where I had parked my car before.

"Hello! How are you?" I inquired of the house owner as he came out to see who had arrived.

"Oh, it's you, teacher," he replied. "You've come again. We are all fine. What about your family?"

With the formalities taken care of, we got down to the business at hand.

"Can I stay in your house tonight?"

"Yes, of course, any time." His eyes wandered over to the three still in the Land Rover.

"And my three friends, too?"

"Yes. Yes. Who are they?"

I explained they were from the German Embassy in Bangkok, which seemed to impress him.

"Oh, yes, two more will be coming later with six cows," which seemed to confuse him a bit.

"Six cows coming here?"

"Well, they can stay outside," I hastily added. "We are sending the cows to the Lahu village up in the hills."

"I see," he said, but I wasn't sure he really did.

We unloaded our bags and drove back into the small town of Mae Suey to eat rice and curry in a little street side restaurant, as we watched evening fall on the quiet dusty streets. We returned to the Thai house, and our hosts gave us tea and fruit. By that time our presence was known by all the neighbors, and the house filled up with people watching the foreigners eat. They stayed and visited with one another and with me. I was thankful, now, for our long, difficult days of language study.

Our hostess put mats down on the floor for us to sleep on, but none of the neighbors got up to leave. Finally, at about 10:00 o'clock, the Ambassador asked me to ask the people to leave because he and his children wanted to undress and go to bed in their sleeping bags. That was probably the moment for which everyone was waiting! I explained to the Ambassador that this was not my house, and I really couldn't ask them to leave. Thais are accustomed to changing clothes and even bathing in public places, however, this is done very modestly. Men wear a loin cloth called a *pakama*, and women wear a sarong called a *pasin*. They bathe in those and change clothes under them without exposing themselves. The Ambassador and his children were not accustomed to that practice. Under the glare of a pressure lantern, they prepared for bed, and crawled into their sleeping bags with most of their clothes on. Privacy in a Thai house is a frame of mind. I waited awhile for the truck and then turned in, concerned about Arno, Hardy and the cattle.

About midnight I heard the truck. I hurriedly threw on some clothes and went out to help unload the cattle. They had brought six cows which we unloaded in the dark and tied to trees around the house. They had arrived late because of difficulty in renting a truck and driver in Chiang Mai. They got a late start, and the old truck had engine trouble along the way. They had stopped several times for repairs during the two hundred kilometer trip. The remainder of the night seemed very short and dawn came early.

When it was light, we started to prepare our packs for the hike. I had sent word ahead for some Lahus to meet us to help carry packs and lead the cows on the four hour hike to their village in the hills. They hadn't arrived yet, but we decided we might as well get started with the cattle, and let the carriers bring the boxes and packs later.

The cattle were still tied to the trees and appeared docile enough, so I put a lead rope around the neck of each one and handed ropes to various people. From then on things became confused. I know I had one cow. Arno and Gunthar had one each. I'm not sure who had the other three, but I assumed they were in the hands of some Lahu villagers who showed up just as we were leaving. As soon as we started, those cows went wild. I've been around cattle most of my life, but I never saw anything like those mavericks. We tried to hold them when they started to run, but we just couldn't manage.

I saw Gunthar having trouble, so told him to hang on. To his credit he did. That cow pulled him through a newly planted rice paddy with the poor boy being dragged along behind on his stomach as if water skiing. He lost his grip on the rope going over an irrigation ditch and received rather bad rope burns on his hands. He was wearing German lederhosen (short leather pants), so his legs were scratched and he was mud from head to toe.

Within ten minutes we had lost all our cows, and they went tearing around the village with people running, dogs barking, and children screaming. Frightened chickens were flying all over. It was a rather large village with the houses well spread out and lots of trees and brush between the houses. The cows were hard to see, much less catch. We chased those cows around and around until we were all exhausted. Finally, we caught four and tied them to trees. The remaining two went hightailing it across the paddy fields, much to the consternation of the field owners. The rice shoots had been carefully planted just a few days earlier.

Those two cows had turned mad and mean. One villager tried to help, and the cow turned on him and butted him in the stomach. He went flying up and landed on his back in the mud and water of the paddy field. Finally, those two animals followed a stream and went off into the jungle. We decided to leave them, and paid a Thai man to keep his eye on them, and catch them if he could. The Lahus said they would return for them later.

Bone weary, dirty, and unhappy, we again started off with four cows, this time being more careful. We had hoped to leave in the morning coolness, but it was now about 10:00 A.M. and a typical hot and humid July day. Every now and then a cow would make a dash for it, but we hung on, sometimes being dragged behind. Lahus, being a mountain tribe people, live in the mountains, so up into the mountains we went. The higher we went the thicker the forest became. Once my cow made a dash for it through the forest. I tripped, but hung on to the rope and was dragged over logs, stumps and up against a tree. Finally, I got the cow stopped, but my camera, which was slung over my shoulder, was never to be the same again.

After gaining considerable altitude, we came to an Akha tribal village. Akha women wear short skirts made from homespun cotton dyed black and ornate headdresses covered with silver ornaments. The men wear black trousers and a pig tail. The trail passed near the village gate, which is really a ceremonial spirit gate. Fertility symbols and other objects used in spirit ceremonies festooned the gate. Our trail went right through the village, and we collected quite a group of onlookers, consisting mostly of screaming children and barking dogs. I was leading my cow some distance ahead of the others when I heard a shout. I turned to see two cows running down the trail with their lead ropes dragging behind. They had gotten scared, made a dash for it, and broken loose. I quickly tied my cow to a tree and hid behind the tree. When the two cows came running by, I stepped out and grabbed the two ropes. Now I can appreciate the meaning of the expression "riding a tiger." Hanging on to two lead ropes, each attached to a run-a-way cow, must be somewhat comparable.

I was running along behind unsuccessfully trying to stop them when ahead I saw a post right where the trail forked. As we went by I wrapped the ropes around the post and snubbed them tight. Fortunately, it was a solid post and it held. The cows were nearly flipped over when they came to the end of their ropes. Instead of calming down, they just got mad and charged me. I ran out beyond the reach of their ropes and sat down for a rest. The remaining cow and its attendant went by on the run. I told him to keep going. The screaming kids and barking dogs were too much for those cows.

I realized I had a problem with those two cows tied to the post. We couldn't get near to untie the ropes without the cows lowering their heads and charging. To add to the confusion, some Akha men came over and they were very agitated. Speaking in the Northern Thai dialect, the leader of the group emphatically said, "You can't leave those cows there. Remove them at once!"

"Why not?" I replied. "They're not hurting anything."

"No, No! That is not a good place. You can't leave them there."

Apparently the post had a function in spirit ceremonies. Living among the Thai and the various Tribal people of the hills, I had become acquainted with their customs and way of life. I knew I had to adjust to their customs. By this time, however, I'm afraid my patience was running a bit thin.

"If you don't want the cows there, you may move them." I replied curtly.

One look at the stomping, snorting cows and they calmed down a bit, although they evidently were still displeased with the fact that cows were tied to that post.

Gunthar and a Lahu had been leading those two cows. I was supposed to be the "expert," so they were waiting for me to suggest something. What I really wanted to do was shoot both cows on the spot and go home. I decided not to share that pleasant thought with my co-sufferers and suggested we have lunch. Gunthar and I had eaten only a few pieces of fried bananas for breakfast, and now it was 4:00 P.M. We had taken the precaution to carry some rice and curry along in plastic bags, but I now discovered that none of the three of us had any of the bags with us. The others had the food and they were far ahead of us. I wished I had never heard of this trip or seen those cows. I did have three small pieces of cold fried banana left which I shared between the three of us.

In the meanwhile, I had been thinking. I needed some bull rings, like the one I had used on the bull at Ban Nawk village. I didn't have any bull rings with me, but there was bamboo growing all around us. I reasoned that we could sharpen a narrow piece of bamboo and use it for the same purpose as a ring. Getting the job done, however, could be a bit dicey

The day was passing. The Akha were getting impatient, and we needed to get to our destination. I borrowed a machete from an Akha villager, cut off a piece of bamboo and split off two pieces about ten inches long, which I sharpened at one end. I gave an extra rope I had in my bag to the Lahu, and told him to give it to me when I called for it. Before the first cow knew what was coming, I stepped up quickly to its side, reached down and grabbed the two legs on her opposite side and pulled. At the same time I leaned on the cow's body with all my might, and down went a surprised cow on its side. Quickly calling for the rope, and with the Lahu helping, we managed to bulldog the cow by tying its legs together. After the cow was safely trussed up, I took the bamboo sliver and thrust it through the cow's nose septum just like putting in a bull ring. I untied the lead rope and tied it to the bamboo nose stick and released the cow's legs. It jumped to its feet, but a slight tug on the rope let it know who was in control now. It allowed itself to be led easily. The other cow was taken care of in a similar fashion, although when I was trying to tie its legs, it gave me a vicious kick which just missed my head and hit my shoulder. I was to have a sore shoulder for several days. Those were small cows, but they were sure wild. They put up more of a struggle than the bull at Ban Nawk.

The second cow reacted differently upon its release. It stood up, walked a few steps, and then refused to budge. Finally, it just lay down and no amount of tail twisting could get it up. Fortunately, it had moved away from the ceremonial post, so we tied it to another tree and told the Akha that someone would come for it the following day. We proceeded on with one less cow. By now we had abandoned three of the six, two back at the starting point and one in the Akha village. One had gone on ahead with the Lahu man. Gunthar and I were left with the two remaining cows. Those two presented us with a new problem. Like us, they were getting tired. They no longer dashed ahead, or turned and charged. Instead they walked slower and slower with frequent stops.

Darkness overtook us when we still were on the trail far from our destination. To add to our misery a light rain began. We were exhausted and hungry. Fortunately, the trail skirted alongside the Karen village of Tung Praow. My work was primarily with Karens and I had been to that village before, so I suggested we spend the night there. We stumbled through the darkness into the village and to the house where I had previously stayed. The mother of the family came out onto the porch of her house.

"*Merga*" (aunty). "Can my friend and I stay in your house tonight?" I explained our situation.

"Of course you can stay. Come up into the house and take a rest." Since I could hardly walk another step, I accepted with alacrity.

Aunty was the mother of a poor family living in a small house constructed of bamboo with a grass thatch roof. Their hospitality, however, was generous. As I lay resting on the front porch, I heard a chicken squawk, and I knew that one of the family's few fowl was being sacrificed to feed us. Hospitality to travelers is customary, but killing a chicken really was special. I was hungry enough to eat it raw, feathers and all, and it was difficult to wait an hour while it was prepared into a proper Karen soup.

Finally, our hostess placed the bowl of soup before us and steaming plates of rice. Never had I approached a meal with such eagerness or with such gratefulness to these people of the mountains who were sharing their livelihood with us. The food was on a low table about ten inches high, and we squatted on the floor around the table. That was customary, but tonight I could not squat. My legs contracted into painful muscle cramps. I ended up sitting on an upturned bucket, and ate my first real meal of the day at 10:00 P.M.

We had carried blankets with us in our back packs, and, after eating, our host spread out reed mats on the porch and on those we spread our blankets and laid down to sleep. I had forgotten how strange all this must seem to Gunthar. He was suffering from a bit of culture shock. Besides, he was wondering what had happened to his father and sister. I assured him that they undoubtedly had gone ahead to the Lahu village with Arno and Hardy which we all had expected to reach easily that day.

As we lay on the porch of the Karen house, I told Gunthar about the Thai people who live in the valleys and practice irrigated rice cultivation, and the Mountain Tribes who live in the hills and plant hill rice in jungle clearings on the steep hillsides. Today we had seen Lahu, Akha and Karen tribal people. In the area were also Lisu, Mien and Hmong. Each group has its own language, customs and dress. They are a unique and wonderful people.

The night passed rapidly, although I slept fitfully because of leg cramps. At dawn the daughters of the house started pounding rice to remove the hulls before cooking. The noise awakened us, so we got up and dressed. For breakfast we were fed the last of the chicken soup and more rice.

Greatly refreshed we took our two cows and proceeded on the trail to the Lahu village of Huey Pu. We arrived after two more hours, and discovered the rest of our party swimming in the Mae Suey River, which was a clear stream originating in those mountains, with jungle vines and creepers hanging from great trees just right for swinging on over the stream. I didn't feel so energetic that day, so just took a leisurely bath. The Ambassador was glad to see his son. He had been worried about him. We went back to the house of a Lahu man named Cai Shen, who was to be responsible for the cattle, to plan the next portion of our trek. I was still stiff and sore and in no mood for a long hike. However, our plan was to continue on in a northerly direction until we hit the Mae Kok River which flows on down to Chiang Rai. At the river we planned to rent a boat to return to that city. It would be about a three day walk to the river through country I had never seen before and the others wanted me along as translator, so I agreed to go. That meant I would have to leave the Land Rover where it was and return for it at a later time by bus.

The cattle delivered to the Lahu village.

Cai Shen sent some men after the cows that had been abandoned. I spent the day resting. Again, we were receiving great hospitality. We not only had chicken and eggs with our rice, but also wild game, such as deer and monkey. That evening we hired five new carriers to accompany us to carry all the things the Ambassador had brought to give to the villagers along the way. I had learned to travel light, but on that trip I had to accommodate the Ambassador. He had previously served in Africa, and distributing gifts along the route of a trek must have been customary. The Lahus who had gone to the Akha village after the cow came back without it. It still wouldn't move. It must have been more tired than I was, or smarter!

The following morning twelve of us left the village for the trek to the Mae Kok River, five Germans, six Lahus, and me. After walking for more than an hour, we came to a Lisu village on Huey Krai Creek. Cai Shen said there was a Chinese Haw (Yunnanese) village about thirty minutes walk to the east. Some of the Yunnanese were remnants of the Chinese Nationalist's 93rd Army, which had found shelter in northern Thailand after their defeat in China. They still maintained contact with Taiwan, and in Thailand are led by two generals, much like the old warlord tradition. They tend to be somewhat suspicious of strangers, and since both Arno and Hardy were carrying hunting rifles, I suggested we continue on the main trail.

After continuing northward for another hour, we came to the Karen village of U Nu, which was a village of twelve houses. The people there had never seen Europeans, and when I spoke to them in Karen, they automatically answered in the Northern Thai dialect, which was their means of communication with the larger world outside their village. When it finally dawned on them that I was speaking their own language, they asked if I was a Karen. I assured them I was not. They wanted medicine, and did not seem to care what kind. I gave them a few aspirin, which was all I had with me. We bought some rice from them, and the Lahus cooked it for our midday meal.

In the middle of the afternoon we met two policemen with a Lisu prisoner. I asked what had happened, so the police stopped to tell me the story. Lisu customarily have a bride price, so when a man wants a bride, he must pay the girl's father an agreed upon amount. That man's daughter had married, but the son-in-law was able to pay only part of the bride price. He had promised to pay the rest later. However, when the father pressed him for the debt, the son-in-law refused to pay any more. The father became so enraged he killed his son-in-law. Now he was docilely on his way to the police station at Mae Suey.

Late in the afternoon we came to the Mien and Red Lahu village of Ju Ji, and decided to spend the night. I think they were rather awed by our large group and by the rifles carried by Arno and Hardy. They were not friendly, but we managed to buy rice and receive permission to stay in a house. We couldn't obtain any meat, but I had two small cans of U. S. Army C-ration meat with me, and we ate those with our rice. After we had eaten, a small group came into the house to stare at us. The Ambassador explained we just were hiking for fun, and that we wanted to leave some presents with them. I translated for him into Northern Thai, and we passed out some gifts of soap, candy, and cloth. That night we weren't provided even with sleeping mats, and I spent a rather uncomfortable night on the uneven split bamboo floor. I did not own a rifle and would not carry one in an area where I was not known. It would only raise suspicions. However, Arno and Hardy wanted to carry their rifles in case we saw some wild game. Perhaps they also wanted to protect the Ambassador and his children from robbers. I did not think that was necessary.

The following morning we decided to leave as soon as we got up since the people were obviously still suspicious of our motives for being there. Opium was grown around there and smuggled out to buyers from the towns, so they may have thought we were narcotic suppression police. We walked on for two more hours to the large Mien and Yunnanese village of Wawi. There we found a store and purchased eggs, dried fish, garlic, and rice. Cai Shen found a building in which to cook it, which was a big barn of a house that was also used to process tea leaves

There were many tea bushes in that area. The villagers said they didn't plant the tea bushes; they just came up. However, it was a rather low quality semi-wild tea. The tea bushes were scattered around on the hillsides and grew quite tall, like trees. Tea is in the Camellia family and the blossoms resemble small camellia flowers. The coarse leaves are picked and pickled in vinegar, which is the *miang*, or pickled tea, which the Northern Thai and Tribal people like to chew. In the market towns it can be bought in large bundles, or in dainty little packets made of banana leaves. Wrapping *miang* in those elaborately prepared packets is a local art form, and is often taught to school children in handicraft classes. *Miang*, along with betel nut and tobacco, is placed in a basket and offered to guests visiting in Northern Thai homes. It is also a part of the hospitality offered at weddings and funerals.

The finer leaves are used for beverage tea, and those were being processed in this primitive processing plant. First, the leaves were wilted and dried in a large pan over a fire, then pressed in a kind of hand press. Finally, the dried leaves were pressed down into gunny sacks and sent to the market towns on pack horses.

We were not in a simple village of farmers, as I first thought. Yunnanese and Mien predominated. The Mien are a tribal group that originated in China and most of them speak Yunnanese, a province in southwest China. The Mien women wore wide trousers with a great deal of cross stitching. It can take up to a year to make a pair of those pants with the elaborate needlework. A large red muff made of yarn extends down the middle of their blouses. A turban nine feet in length, also heavily embroidered, is wrapped around their heads. There were also some Red Lahu and Karens living in the village. Tea and opium are important local industries, which likely explained why there was such an ethnic mix in this village.

The Thai government also maintained a Border Police school there. Border Police are sent to villages like this where they are the representatives of the Thai government. They provide police protection, arbitrate in local conflicts, run a simple medical clinic, and teach school. They are also the eyes and ears of the government in those remote border villages. As strangers, we would be of interest to them, so we presented ourselves at the station and chatted for a while. In areas such as this, the Border Police are accepted better than the regular police. They provide services and have received some training in how to live and work among the Tribal people. In order to be accepted, they left the opium trade pretty much alone.

Many of the Chinese houses in the village had walls made of mud. I had never seen mud-wall houses in Thailand before. That type of house construction is similar to the village houses in some parts of China. Larger houses had an open courtyard in the middle.

After eating, we proceeded on and started climbing up rather steep hills. After about two hours, we reached the top of the divide separating the Mae Kok and the Mae Suey River systems. It was beautiful country, and the air was cooler because of the elevation. Due to its elevation, pine trees grew there, and their fragrance filled the air. On top of the ridge we came to another large Mien and Yunnanese village called Ban Kiew. It was in a large opium growing and trading area. Just before the village, we crossed a large, heavily traveled trail going east and west. Cai Shen told me that was the trail on which the drug is taken to the district town of Fang where it enters the illicit international drug pipeline. It was best not to ask too many questions or take pictures of the numerous poppy fields now being prepared.

Yunnanese pack horses.

Opium is more of a temperate climate crop, so in Thailand it can be grown only in the higher elevations. Usually, a field of corn was planted first on a hillside clearing toward the end of April, when the rains began. The tiny poppy seeds are sowed as soon as the corn is harvested in July. Most tropical soils tend to be a bit too acid for the poppy, but experienced farmers will search out plots of land suitable for planting the poppies. Often this will be below some limestone cliffs, where the soil is less acid. Some people have told me they are able to "taste" the soil to determine if it is good for opium or not. The corn stalks provide protection to the fragile opium seedlings as they grow during the heaviest rainfall months of August and September.

One of the prettiest sights I have ever seen were fields of opium poppy in full bloom on the high hills and ridges of north Thailand. One is sobered, however, by the misery that comes forth from that beauty. The poppy blossoms in December and January and as soon as the petals begin to fall, but while the seed pods are still green and sappy, the grower will make a scratch with a three-bladed knife on the seed pod. A sticky sap exudes from those wounds, which is collected the following day by scraping it off with a flat knife blade. That is the raw opium. It is collected in a ball, like a brown ball of wax. That all requires a lot of hand labor, so the opium planting tribes, such as the Mien, Hmong, and Lisu, desire large families.

The opium is collected in large balls which each have a weight of one *joi* (1.6 kilograms). One *joi* was selling for about $250.00 at the time of our trek. Smaller amounts of raw opium may be used like currency; so much weight for a basket of rice, or so much for hiring a day laborer. Even people who never use or plant it will accept it as currency. The raw opium can be smoked as it is, and many of the Tribal people become addicted to it. Most of it, however, is refined into heroin and smuggled throughout the world.

Hmong lady tending her opium field.

Two men smoking opium.

Akha women and child removing seeds from opium poppy seed pods.

We stopped for a rest in that village and sat on a bench outside a small store. The Ambassador bought canned laichi fruit for all of us. I noticed the cans came from Hong Kong. There were no roads in that area, so everything from the outside must be carried in on horseback or on people's backs. Not surprisingly, the price was rather high.

From there the trail forked, one fork going northwest to the Lahu village of Huey Hawm on the Mae Kok River and one going northeast to the Lahu village of Kok Noi, and on to the Mae Kok River. I had been to both of those villages when traveling by boat on the Mae Kok River. We decided to go to Kok Noi, which is located on a stream of the same name.

It started to rain, but we continued on, although it was very difficult going downhill on the slippery trail. Spills were frequent and we were soon soaked and muddy. We saw some Mien field houses a short way off the trail and went over to get out of the rain. The Ambassador was behind us, and we all assumed one carrier had stayed with him. However, we counted heads at the field house and discovered we were all there, except the Ambassador. I had visions of the Ambassador being lost in the hills and rain. Soon, however, he came strolling in smoking his pipe. He had seen the houses and assumed it was our destination. During World War II the Ambassador was a colonel in the German Army and had survived three years on the Russian Front. He could take care of himself!

Cai Shen said it should take one and a half hours from Ban Kiew to Kok Noi. It took us four hours. I was beginning to think we were on the wrong trail. The rain and slippery trail slowed us down some, but not that much. I think it would take three hours under good conditions. We finally arrived late in the afternoon, in time to take a bath in the stream and wash our muddy clothes. We all stayed in the headman's house, which was not very large. We nearly filled it. The people of this village knew me, and we were received with great friendliness.

The villagers had planted lots of corn and they brought a large basket of roasting ears to the house. True happiness is sitting around a fire in dry clothes listening to rain on the thatch roof while you roast and eat ears of corn. The Ambassador and his children had never eaten corn before. In Europe corn was considered to be only animal feed. Animal feed or not, they enjoyed the corn.

Lahu houses usually have two fireplaces, one in the kitchen and one in the main living room. They are simply open fires built on an earth filled box set into the floor. The smoke just goes up and filters through the grass thatch roof. Usually, a drying platform is suspended over the fire for drying meat, fish, chili peppers, seed, or whatever. Ears of corn to be used for seed are suspended from the roof over the fire. The smoking process prevents weevil damage. Guests, like us, stay in the living room. A sooty old teapot was put on the fire to make tea. We sat on the floor sipping hot tea, eating corn and resting up from that day's trek.

The grass thatch roofs of those houses really are wonderful. They are made of only a thin layer of imperata grass tied to pieces of bamboo and put on like shingles. Daylight can be seen through the grass, so there is ventilation and smoke passes through easily, yet they do not leak when it rains.

We were tired from our previous two days walking, so decided to stay another day. Someone reported seeing the tracks of a sambur deer near the village, which is a large deer, nearly as large as the North American elk. I borrowed a rifle from a villager, which turned out to be an old U. S. Army M-1 Carbine, and Arno and I went hunting. We didn't see anything but a saucy squirrel, who scolded us from a bamboo clump.

Our host had shot a porcupine two days before, and it was cut up and drying on the drying platform. We had it for supper the second day in the form of a curry. It was delicious. It tasted like wild pig, or even better. I had been to this village in January, and some hunters brought in a wild boar. They didn't shoot it, but had surprised a tiger that had just killed the boar. They shot at the tiger and missed, but the tiger ran away leaving the boar. The hunters confiscated the pig. It was dark by the time they finished dressing it out, so they stayed where they were and built a big fire. They stayed awake all night, half expecting the tiger to come back to reclaim the prize. I had eaten some of that pig, and now I was here again eating porcupine. The flavor was similar.

The hunters bringing back the meat of a wild pig killed by a tiger.

Kok Noi was a poor village. They had no paddy fields, only hill fields. They were a simple, unsophisticated people who had come from a remote area of Burma. Their hospitality was real, however, and we enjoyed their company. Sitting around the fire our host, who spoke Northern Thai dialect, regaled us with tales of his experiences in the Burmese Army. He told of one expedition to the Wa people along the Burma-China border. Those people are sometimes called the "Wild Wa of Burma." They were headhunters up until rather recent times. According to our host, the Wa collected the heads of some Japanese soldiers during World War II. Anyway, two things had impressed him about the Wa people. He said they didn't wear much clothes, and they raised large numbers of pigs.

In talking about the various kinds of people in that part of the world, I asked about a group the Thai call the *Phi Tong Luang* (Spirits of the Yellow Leaves). He was not acquainted with the Thai name, but when I described the group as being a people who did not plant anything, but simply gathered food and hunted in the forest, he knew what I meant. He called them *Khon Pa* (forest people). He said he had seen them in Burma. They live in the deep forest and never make permanent villages, but move about from place to place hunting and gathering. He said he had seen only the men, never women or children. The Lahus are great hunters, but our host praised the hunting ability of those "wild men." They don't have guns, but the men smear the blood and manure from a wild pig all over their bodies and hide by a game trail. They may have to wait all day, but when a wild pig comes by they spear it. Apparently, the wild game are not able to detect their human odor.

There were some areas near the village of Kok Noi that would be suitable for making the irrigated rice paddies. In fact, someone apparently had developed them at one time many years ago, but they had grown over with brush and trees. I asked the headman about those old fields.

"Why aren't the people in this village clearing and planting rice in those old terraced rice paddies? That would be better than making hill fields every year."

"We would really like to use them", the headman replied, "but they are owned by some Mien people higher up in the mountains. We would have to buy them."

"Why don't you buy them?"

"We have no money."

"Are they expensive?"

"They would cost 10,000 baht ($500)."

That really was inexpensive, but I knew he spoke the truth. They did not have money, except for bare essentials. I translated that conversation to the Ambassador and he revealed that the German Embassy had a small fund that could be used for charity or development projects.

"The Ambassador might be able to help," I told the headman.

"That would be wonderful. Some of the families here are thinking of leaving because there is not even enough good land for hill fields."

"Is 10,000 baht really enough?"

"Yes, that is enough for the land."

"What about water buffaloes? You would need some to plow the paddy fields."

"We could probably get by with two. Do you mean the Ambassador would help with the buffalo too?"

The Ambassador decided the Embassy Fund could help with 12,000 baht, which would be adequate to purchase the land and two buffalo.

"As soon as I return to Bangkok I will send the money to Mr. Nelson," the ambassador told the headman. "He will deliver it to you."

That news was received with great joy by the headman and the other villagers sitting around the fire. Our teacups were refilled and more corn put on the fire. About a month later I did return to that village with the money. The land and buffalo were bought, and to this day the people in the Lahu village of Kok Noi proudly farm their irrigated rice paddies.

The following day was Sunday and this was a Christian village. Arno and I attended an early church service at 6:00 a.m. There was no pastor in the village, but the Scripture was read, hymns sung, and someone volunteered a brief devotion. One of the men who led the service had shared our conversation the night before around the fire. He was a strong, robust man of about forty-five years of age. I had met him previously and knew he had two wives. Local Thai villagers called him *Nai Sawng Mia* (Mr. Two Wives). In his house were three women; his elderly mother, his first wife, and a younger wife. They were an exceedingly hard working family. The man and his two wives worked hard in the fields. The old mother kept house and baby-sat. Somehow, in that setting, it did not seem strange to see him leading a Christian service. He was a good man. He honored God and his fellow man, worshipped his Creator and worked hard to care for his family.

After breakfast, Cai Shen and one carrier returned to their village. The rest of us continued on. We walked another hour to the Red Lahu village of Haad Yao on the Mae Kok River, and took a ferry boat across the river to the Christian Yellow Lahu village of Aw Swaeng. We were in time for the main church service, held at midday. Again Arno and I attended. Like in the other village, the church was constructed of bamboo and grass thatch, similar to their houses. Split logs were the pews. Men sat on one side and women on the other.

We spent the night there, and on Monday morning rented a boat to take us up the river. It was a typical river boat, long and narrow with the propeller on the end of a long shaft extending out of the end of the boat. We went as far as the Lahu village of Wanglee and the Shan village of Ban Mai. There was another Border Police station and school at Wanglee. A policeman told us that the first American astronauts had arrived on the surface of the moon. They had just heard the news on their radio. It was July 21, 1969. I will never forget where I was on that day. The Germans all congratulated me, since I was the only American around.

There were two young Border Policemen stationed at Wanglee. One was absent, so I chatted with the one left in the village. He cradled his M-16 rifle in his lap as he told me his story. He came from Bangkok, and was first sent to a Mien village near the Laos border. He established a school for village children and provided some medical care. One night a villager woke him up and told him to flee immediately as the Communist terrorists were coming to kill him. He was running away, barefooted and in his underwear, when he was shot at and one bullet went through his shoulder. He managed to continue running and made his escape. He unbuttoned his shirt and showed me an ugly scar, not yet properly healed. He had been transferred to this village, which was relatively quiet and safe.

The Border Policeman at Wanglee Village.

We returned back down stream stopping at numerous villages along the way. Villagers apparently had been hearing about us and gave us gifts. We were given sixteen eggs and two parakeets. When we arrived back at Aw Swaeng, Hardy and I made scrambled eggs using the sixteen eggs, one tin of corned beef, and five Chinese sausages. Not bad! We ate it with rice. In that village they played the Lahu gourd flutes that sound like bagpipes, and gave us a demonstration of a sword dance.

We stayed there another night and in the morning caught a passenger boat going downstream to Chiang Rai. It rained most of the way, and the boat had no roof. We arrived in Chiang Rai at 9:00 a.m., and walked through town to a restaurant that served a Western breakfast of fried eggs and toast. We created a considerable amount of interest parading through town in our wet clothes, back packs, and Arno and Hardy with their uncased rifles. We enjoyed a breakfast without rice and returned to our house. Dee already knew we had arrived in town. She had been in the market when people told her, "Your husband has just arrived with a group of foreigners and hill tribesmen." We couldn't surprise her. The Germans cleaned up, changed clothes, and took the plane out at noon.

In the afternoon the carriers and I went back to Mae Suey by bus to get my Land Rover. We found out that the two cows left there were so wild they couldn't be caught. The Lahus had shot them like deer and sold the meat. The one left in the Akha village had finally consented to be led. Four out of the six cows had made it. Two of those were heavy with calf, so soon there would be six.

Five Germans and one American had a trip they would never forget. We had met people who had befriended us, taken care of us, and showed us another world. Far out in space a man had walked on the moon. All of us on that trek, the Lahus from Burma, the Germans and the American, had a bit of the moon walker in them. To go to new places, forge new trails and see strange sights is all part of our human experience. Actually, I wouldn't have traded places with that moon walker. I think I had the better experience; certainly the more human one. To argue with Akha, trek with Lahu, bathe in clear cold streams, eat corn on the cob around a fire, get to know Mr. Two Wives, accept gifts of eggs from kind people, and worship our Creator in the morning stillness were all real and valuable experiences which knit us together in our common humanity. Meeting and knowing people made a simple trek across the hill country of northern Thailand a warm and memorable experience.

WHAT I LEARNED AT
NAMLAT SCHOOL

Sahasatsuksa School at Namlat village was growing. I had obtained funding from Church sources to build a dormitory and four new classrooms. The school already had Karen, Lahu and a few Northern Thai students, but now other Tribal parents wanted to send their children to that school, so we accepted Hmong, Mien, and Lisu students. The teachers said, "We have our own United Nations right here." Those students from the ethnic minorities did not speak the Thai language, so usually spent two years in first grade. After one year their language ability was good, and they could proceed on through the seventh grade of that elementary school. All of those new students came from some distance and were boarding students staying in the dormitories, even those who were six or seven years old. Adult house parents were hired to live in the dormitories and provide supervision. Dr. Tom Roberts, a missionary doctor at Overbrook Hospital in Chiang Rai, saw the potential of the school and provided funding to purchase additional land and build another dormitory

Temporary dormitory made from bamboo with grass thatch roof.

New dormitory at the school, 1971.

One year the Akha village of Huey San sent six little boys and girls to the school. I believe they were the first Akha children in Thailand to go to school. Their parents brought them to the school, and there was a lot of crying when it was time for them to leave. The children weren't crying, their mothers were!

It was my idea to put double-bunk beds in the new girl's dormitory. That was an American concept. In the Thai situation, it was not a good idea. At home everybody sleeps on the floor. We discovered the children were falling out of their beds at night. The very first night of that new school year one Akha girl fell out of her upper bunk. Unfortunately, she was on the second floor and right next to an open window. She rolled off the bed and right out the window. Khru Pipat, a teacher living in a nearby house, heard the sound of her body hitting the ground and went out to investigate. He found the little girl lying unconscious on the ground.

He took her to Overbrook Hospital, somehow managing to hold her with one hand while he drove his motorcycle with the other hand. She returned to consciousness at the hospital, and the doctors could find no injuries, so Khru Pipat returned her to the dormitory and told her to sleep on the floor.

Word of that incident reached the parents at Huey San village. The fathers of the Akha children, sent by their wives, returned to take their children home where it was safer. However, the teachers convinced the Akha men that such an accident would never happen again, and the children could sleep on the floor. The father of the girl who had fallen stayed on another day and constructed a kind of crib out of old wood for his daughter to sleep in. He was taking no chances, either with his daughter or his wife!

The Akha children stayed in school, and did very well. They learned Thai that first year and became excellent students. One of the girls became the top student in the whole school, and later graduated from Chiang Mai University. Many more Akha children followed them, and they became the largest ethnic group in the school. Two of the children who came that first year were a little boy and his older sister. The older sister was only 18 months older than her brother, but the teachers allowed the boy to stay in the girl's dormitory with his sister, so she could help look after him. Years later I went to that boy's wedding. I reminded his bride that her husband was the only boy who had lived in the girl's dormitory!

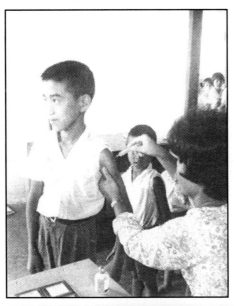

Akha student receiving an inoculation from a volunteer nurse.

Several Hmong students started attending the school after their families had been relocated by the Thai Government. They had been living in a mountainous place near the Mae Khong River. Some Hmong from that area were in conflict with government authorities and had received weapons from Communist guerillas infiltrating from Laos. The Thai Army relocated some of the peaceful villagers to Payao, a district south of Chiang Rai, and some of their children came to our school.

One of the Hmong students contracted encephalitis during the rainy season, and was in a coma at the hospital for eight days. His father sat by his side the entire time. Sometimes I joined him and we prayed together for his son. The doctors didn't think he would survive, and would be brain damaged if

123

he did because of his high fever. He did survive, and although he was a bit slow for a few weeks, his full mental capacity did return. The doctors were surprised. The boy's father, however, only smiled.

Some of the students had malaria when they arrived, but responded to treatment. Overbrook Hospital provided worm medicine free of charge, so twice a year Dee and I brought several large bottles to the school; enough to dose every child. Encephalitis, however, was the most feared disease. It was spread by mosquitoes, so came with the rainy season when there were puddles of water everywhere. I borrowed mechanical foggers from the Public Health Department and sprayed insecticide around the school to kill the mosquitoes. Still, the following year, after the Hmong student's illness, A Lahu boy contracted the disease. His father came from a distant village to be with him, but the boy died in the hospital after falling into a coma. He was buried at the burial place for Namlat Village. Heavy rains had caused the grave to fill with water, so the wooden coffin floated, until muddy soil was heaped on top of it to weight it down. It was a sad occasion for all, including the entire student body who attended the burial service. I continued the spraying program, and no more students contracted encephalitis.

Although I had no official capacity, I was not pleased with the amount of time I had to spend at the school. I was supposed to be doing agricultural and village development work. What was I doing building dormitories and sitting on lengthy school committee meetings? Inevitably, there were conflicts between teachers and parents. Most of the teachers were Thai, but the school was located in a Karen village, and there were cultural differences. If a teacher punished a Karen student I soon heard about it from the Karens. *"Thra,"* they told me, "My son is not treated fairly at that school. The Thai teachers are too severe with him because he is a Karen." So, I would have to be the "middle man" and take the parent's complaint to the teacher.

"No way," the teacher would exclaim. "We are always fair. That boy was making a disturbance in class."

Being the resident missionary I was dragged into controversies. "Whatever you say, *Thra*, we'll do whatever you say." What they really meant, was that I should follow their point of view. I hated being a judge. Usually, I suggested they bring the matter up at the next school committee meeting. The school committee was something like a school board, composed mostly of village men and one or two teachers. During our first few years in Chiang Rai I approached those meetings with dread. Sometimes I couldn't even sleep the night before a meeting.

I soon learned, however, that the Thais and Karens did not like confrontation either. They wanted to avoid conflict. It was enough for the complainers, either Thai or Karen, to voice their complaint. The other side would make conciliatory statements, and peace would prevail. Until the next issue came up!

I did learn a lot about working with the village people. The head teacher was Khru Arom, a local Northern Thai. Khru Arom was a good teacher and a good administrator. He was honest and fair. However, he had one fault. He was the most undiplomatic Thai person I ever met. He spoke too plainly. If he thought somebody was lazy he would say so, no matter whose feelings he hurt. Also, he did not spend much time visiting with the villagers, and as a result was not well liked.

The village people on the school committee decided they wanted to hire another teacher, not head teacher, just a regular teacher. He was also Northern Thai, but was well liked. I knew what the committee wanted. They wanted to reduce the authority of Khru Arom. They wanted someone they liked to be a counterweight to him. I was acquainted with the teacher they wanted to hire. He was a heavy drinker and was fired from his previous teaching position because of a financial scandal. The villagers didn't like teachers who drank. They didn't like people who stole money, but they liked that man. They liked him because he obviously liked them. He would spend time in their homes just telling stories and having a good time. He got along with people.

So, there was another school committee meeting. I knew what the main agenda item was going to be, but everything else was discussed first. Finally, the proposal to hire that teacher came up. I thought he would be a disaster, but kept my opinion to myself. I thought the committee should reach a decision without depending on me. The meeting went on and on for two more hours. Finally, the committee chairman, who was a village headman from another Karen village, said, "Well, if *Thra* Nelson is not going to say yea or nay we will not hire him. Meeting adjourned." It had been a tense meeting, and I was exhausted. I was late for supper. "Where have you been?" Dee asked. "Don't you know when to come home and eat?" "It was a long meeting," was all I could say.

From that episode with the teacher I learned the importance of spending time in the villages talking to people. They liked that. They wanted to tell me about their families. It helped me become close to them. That, in turn, made it easier for me to introduce agricultural and community development projects. However, I was also conflicted within. "Daddy," Lani and Rebecca would say, "you're gone a lot." Yes, I was gone a lot, maybe too much.

I also had another function at the school that took a lot of time. The boarding students started receiving aid from an organization in the United States that sponsors children of poor families. All our students qualified. Each sponsor contributed a monthly stipend to the child they were sponsoring. Each child had to write letters to their sponsor, and many sponsors wrote to their child. It really was a good program, and very helpful to our boarding students. However, I got stuck with translating all the letters. The students wrote their letters in Thai, so I would translate each one into English and send them back to the supporting organization to be sent on to each sponsor.

When the sponsors wrote back to their child I would usually translate that orally to the student. It was faster that way. Translating all the student's letters, however, became a time consuming burden, especially when the number of sponsored students exceeded 100. I maintained my village trips, and most evenings sat at my desk translating those letters. One good thing, however, was that I got acquainted with the students through their letters. They wrote about their families, always mentioning their own birth order, such as "I am number three of seven children." They may have been ethnic minorities from poor, remote villages, but they had dreams for their future. Many wanted to become school teachers. Eventually, the school hired a Karen lady who was able to do the translating. It was a load off my back, but I kind of missed those letters too.

During the time we lived in Chiang Rai I considered the time spent with school related matters as something extra that had been pushed on me without my consent. I was there, so I had to do it. However, years later looking back over my Thailand experience I realize it was also an educational experience for me, and I know that the work I did at Sahasatsuksa School was the most useful thing I have ever done. Hundreds of Tribal children received an education, helped their families, became community and church leaders and became useful citizens of the Kingdom of Thailand.

Porntip, a Lahu student at Sahasatsuksa School.

Rupert with teachers at Sahasatsuksa School
About 1967.

Morning flag raising ceremony at the opening of school.

Boarding school students eating their dinner.

COMMUMIST INSURGENCY

During the 1960's and 70's there was some Communist insurgency in northern Thailand. The war in Vietnam was growing and spilling into Laos and Cambodia, Thailand's neighbors. The Thai news media was censored by the military government at that time. Newspapers were allowed to print bad news about the Communists, such as raids on rural police stations and assassinations of local leaders, but could not print some of the injustices inflicted on the poor and minority people living in the hills that caused them to retaliate, or seek help from people who had weapons, the Communists.

It was a time of political unrest. People were afraid. Many Thais believed the "domino theory" was a possibility. First Vietnam, Laos, Cambodia, and maybe even Thailand. Such fears bred more oppression. Labor unions and farmer's organizations were banned. Politicians who professed "socialist tendencies" were persecuted. Some were jailed and others fled the country. Government leaders feared poor rural people, who may have been influenced by "Leftists". Sometimes village people, especially in Northeast Thailand near Laos, feared government officials who responded harshly to calls for economic and social justice. There was not much real communication between those two elements.

We were advised by our Mission organization to keep our Landrover gas tank full, and keep an extra can of gasoline on hand, in case a hasty evacuation was needed. I didn't think that would happen, but followed instructions, just to be safe.

Police and government workers did have some legitimate concerns. Sometimes they would be shot if they were in rural areas, or mountain villages. Maybe they were shot by Communist sympathizers, or maybe by people who had suffered from corrupt officials. Times were changing. People were very much aware that a peasant army in Vietnam could not even be defeated by a superpower.

During that time I asked the Government Fisheries Department in Chiang Rai if they could help develop some fish ponds in a Karen village that was only about 20 kilometers out of town; the same village where Swe Po and I had carried in the lychi trees. They said they could go, so I agreed to take them in my Landrover. When I went to pick them up, they had arranged for three policemen, armed with rifles, to go with us. They were afraid to go without an armed escort, even to a peaceful Karen village. I wouldn't take the police.

"You don't need protection to go to this village," I told them. "I go there all the time. They're good people." Somewhat sheepishly, they told the police they were not needed. I did not want a police escort. The village people trusted me, and I trusted them. However, that was a typical attitude of civil servants. If they had been close to the people, they would have no reason to be afraid.

The area to the east of us, between Chiang Rai and the Mae Khong River, did have recurring problems with insurgents. Upon the request of the Thai Government, American Seabees came and built an all season road from Chiang Rai to Chiang Khong. It was considered a strategic road for military purposes, but also helped us when we drove to Chiang Khong and crossed the Mae Khong River to Laos for Dee's immigration trips. However, we never drove that road at night. I almost always got a flat tire going to Chiang Khong, and another one on the return trip. The punctures were caused by pieces of sharp metal that had been placed on the road, an inexpensive form of sabotage.

There were some Hmong villages in the mountains near the Mae Khong River. To make their hill fields they moved around, sometimes in Laos and sometimes in Thailand. They had had some bad experiences with corrupt Thai police and government officials, who extorted money from them. When ordered to leave and return to Laos, they refused. A confrontation occurred, and they shot some policemen. The Hmong were an independent group of mountain people who did not want any government telling them what to do. They also had good weapons and lots of ammunition. I don't think they were really Communists, but they didn't mind receiving help from them. They had new M-16 rifles, which the American Military had given to the Lao Army. Many of the Laotian soldiers promptly sold their rifles to anyone willing to buy them. I sometimes saw M-16s and Russian made Kalishinkov rifles in Tribal villages that were used for hunting. The villagers paid 5,000 Baht for them, which was about $250. The proxy war between Russia and America had unexpected results in the whole region.

Anyway, Thailand sent in their army, complete with artillery, to remove the Hmong. They would not move, and many Thai soldiers lost their lives. Those soldiers said their lives were only worth one old rubber tire, because one tire produced enough heat to cremate one dead soldier. The Thai Air force was even used to bomb the Hmong villages. They used the Chiang Rai Airport, and one of those planes lost a bomb on the middle of the runway when taking off. It did not explode, but the airport was closed for several days until experts were called in to defuse the bomb and remove it. Scheduled Thai Airways flights were not able to land during that time.

One wing of the government hospital in Chiang Rai was used only for wounded Thai soldiers. The Hmong were tough. However, there was another group of tough soldiers located at Doi Maesalong, a remote mountain area north of Chiang Rai. Those were the remnants of Chiang Kai Shek's Chinese Nationalist Army, who had retreated into Burma, and later to Thailand, when they were defeated in China. They made a good living in the illicit drug trade and had no desire to join their compatriots in Taiwan. There were rumors of an arrangement whereby the Thai government allowed the Chinese to stay in their mountain camps, support themselves in the drug trade and be an anti-Communist barrier along the northern border. The Thai military government called on them to remove the recalcitrant Hmong. The Chinese solders were transported in a convoy of trucks at night, passing through Chiang Rai. They attacked the Hmong in their mountain hideouts and drove them out of Thailand, but suffered many casualties.

Most of the Hmong people were not involved in the fighting. They just wanted to be left alone without government interference. However, many of the Hmong near the Laotian border were considered by the Thai government to be "red". Some villages were forcibly removed from the mountains and brought down to lowland areas where they could be easily controlled. One day I went by the police station in Chiang Rai and noticed a large group of Hmong women and children in the yard around the station. They were very upset, and some were weeping bitterly.

"What's going on here," I asked someone passing by.

"Listen," he said.

I listened, and soon realized what was happening. Their men were being interrogated inside the police station. It was not a soft interrogation. Shouted questions and sounds of beatings came through the wooden walls of the station. The women and children were there for two days listening to those sounds. Fear replaced reason. The Thai government feared what they perceived to be a Communist threat. Villagers learned to fear the wrath of police and military.

A few Christian Hmong were among those relocated to Payao, a town south of Chiang Rai. They sent their children to Sahasatsuksu School. They were good students, and already spoke the Thai language because they had been in school at their previous location. One time I had borrowed a large jack to lift up a small house at the school to make foundation repairs. As I was leaving the school in my Landrover I saw one of the teachers and asked him to, *"Gep mae raeng wai di di,"* which means to put the jack away in a good place. A student overheard me, and thought I said, *"Gep Meo Daeng wai di di,"* which means to put the Red Meo (Hmong) away in a good place. Thankfully, the teacher explained to him I was talking about the jack, not Communist Hmong.

I, and other missionaries, were always able to travel freely at that time, although there were areas where Thai government people dared not go. Some government agencies used Landrovers that were the same color as those used by the Baptist missionaries. That was a bit of a worry, because government Landrovers were sometimes shot at. We had a solution: We had a yellow band painted across both sides of our Landrovers to make them look different. I'm not sure if it made a difference, but it made us feel safer. The stripes were soon noticed by other mission groups and non-governmental agencies. "You Baptists all have a yellow streak!" they joked.

University students in Bangkok began to protest against the military government and Thailand's involvement with the United States in the war in Viet Nam. Some became rather radical in their demands for the removal of the leaders of the government, and for free elections. The students gained some sympathy from the population at large, and that was of concern to the military government. A military owned radio station in Bangkok began broadcasting propaganda about the students, accusing them of being Communists and disloyal to His Majesty The King. Those broadcasts caused a mob of Thai people to gather around one university, where a student demonstration was being held, and break in through the gates. They had believed the radio broadcasts and were enraged at the students for being disloyal. Many students were beaten by the mob, and there were reports of some being killed. Police were present, but did not intervene. A nationwide crackdown on students immediately followed that event. Leaders of the demonstrations, and anyone considered to have socialist tendencies were jailed. Many of the students fled to the hills where they tried to join the insurgents. Most were not Communists, but simply agitating for a more democratic government. They wanted justice. In the hill villages they started schools for children and provided some development assistance. Some groups were armed, and did shoot military and police who came looking for them.

They were known as *noksyksa*, which means university students. Attitudes toward them were split. Some Thai people tolerated, or even supported, them. Others thought they were a threat to the nation and should be imprisoned, or even killed. During those difficult days, some Karens told me about a poor Karen village in Maehongsorn Province. The villagers had cut down a few teak trees to construct houses. Teak is protected and it is illegal to cut down teak trees without permission from the Forestry Department. It was, however, permissible for villagers to use teak wood for building their own houses. Officials from the Forestry Department came to the village to arrest the men for cutting down the trees. Suddenly, armed *noksyksa* appeared and gave the government officials a lecture on justice. They reminded the officials that great quantities of teak trees were cut illegally by wealthy and influential people who bribed the officials. "Why are you bothering these poor people who cut a few trees for their own use," they wanted to know. "Now get out of here before we shoot you all." The officials left and never came back. It was not surprising that the students did receive some local support.

His Majesty The King, had a moderating influence. Although he did not have political power, he was greatly loved and respected by all Thais. I once attended a seminar in Chiang

Mai, sponsored by the Forestry Department, concerning the condition of Thai forests. His Majesty opened the seminar, and made some rather pointed remarks. He said "I have visited some Karen villages in the upper Mae Chaem River area (Musikee in Karen), and found large areas of pine forests are being maintained without Forestry Department input. Why is it that Karen villagers can protect their forests, but the Forestry

Department is unable to do the same in other areas?" The Director General of the Forestry Department was present. That must have been hard for him to hear. To be critized by the King was about the worst thing that could happen to a Thai.

His Majesty also related another incident that took place in Prachuap Kirikan Province. A Karen village had their land stolen by corrupt Land Department officials, who colluded with a wealthy and influential person to nullify the traditional land ownership of the village and give a title deed to the wealthy man. The villagers were upset by that action and shot at tractor operators who came to plow their land. The village men were arrested and accused of being Communist insurgents. His Majesty said, "They were not Communists; they just wanted justice." The King has earned the love and respect of his people.

A few years later a more moderate government took over and changed the policy from armed confrontation to trying to win the hearts and minds of the insurgents. That worked. The insurgents came out of the hills and surrendered their weapons. In return, they were given a plot of land to farm, material to build a house, schools were provided, and even food for one year while they were getting established in their new location. The students returned to their families and continued their education. Some even entered government service. Thai people are able to forgive.

I heard some interesting comments from Karen villagers. "Look at us; we have always been peaceful and loyal to Thailand. Now we get nothing, and the Hmong, who fought the government, receive lots of help. It's not fair." Maybe it wasn't, but the immediate problem of Communist inspired insurgency ended.

LANI AND REBECCA: GROWING UP IN THAILAND

Our children have good memories of Thailand, and as adults still enjoy Thai food and like to return to Thailand to see where they grew up. They rapidly became bi-lingual, and functioned well in both Thai and Farang environments. In a mixed group, they would speak Thai to a Thai face and English to a Western face, switching easily from one to he other. On one visa trip to Malaysia, when we were still living in Bangkok, Lani was a bit frustrated because Malay people did not respond to her spoken Thai. They looked like Thai, so she thought they should speak Thai.

Lani attended first and second grades at Chiang Rai Widayakhome School and Rebecca attended a government kindergarten. Most of their early education, however, was with Calvert Correspondence School, with their mother as their home teacher. Calvert mailed us textbooks, curriculum guides, and graded papers sent back to them. It worked, but sometimes it was a strain, on both the girls and their mother.

Rupert Nelson

Lani, second from right, and some other first grade students at
Chiang Rai Widiyakhome School .

Rebecca, seated in center, going by pedicab to her kindergarten.

Flag raising ceremony at Rebecca's kindergarten.

The house we moved into in 1968, after a furlough in the U.S.

They read a lot of books, listened to records and played with their cats, rabbits and dogs. Rebecca bathed her cats in the bathtub and dressed them in doll clothe. Her cats were quite tolerant! They also spent time with our Thai maid who did the laundry, cleaned the house and gave the girls their baths. Her name was Bin. They called her *Pi Bin*, which means elder-sister Bin. After eating at our table they would sometimes sneak out to Bin's room and eat some of the sticky rice she had brought for her lunch. Bin also brought *miang*, which is tea leaves pickled in vinegar. Northern Thai people liked to chew *miang*, like some Americans chew tobacco. *Miang* was often served to guests and when we were in Thai or Tribal homes Lani and Rebecca knew what to do. They would put a cud in their cheek, and slowly chew it like they had lived there all their lives.

Rebecca with her Siamese cat.

Lani holding a pet rabbit in front of bamboo playhouse.

Most small shops in Thailand are open in the evening, so we often took a walk down the main street of Chiang Rai after our evening meal. Shop owners would be sitting on chairs outside the open door of their shops enjoying the evening air. They often engaged us in conversation.

"Nice to see you again. Have you eaten yet?" (literally, have you eaten rice).

"Yes," we replied, "We've eaten already. What about you?"

"We ate already. Thank you."

"Have you eaten yet?" was a common greeting all over Thailand. Next, they would turn to Lani and Rebecca.

"Well, look at your daughters, they are growing very fast."

The girls knew what to do next; they would *wai* (Thai curtsy) very nicely.

"Oh, *na rak, na rak* (cute). I have some *canoms* (sweets) for them."

The girls were quite shameless, and successfully tried that trick over and over. They knew they had a good thing going!

Barbequed meat stand in Chiang Rai

Beginning with the fourth grade Lani attended the Chiang Mai Co-educational Center, a school in Chiang Mai that used English as the medium of instruction. She lived in a boarding house provided for children of missionaries and other expatriate children. It was a 30 minute plane ride to Chiang Mai, or an 11 hour drive by Land Rover, so we didn't see much of her, except at school vacations. She was very brave to live away from home at such an early age. It helped that she was together with several friends of the same age. Later, we moved to Chiang Mai, so the girls could live at home and attend that school. They attended high school at International School, Bangkok, again living in a boarding house.

Lani and Rebecca often accompanied us on village trips, usually a day trip, but sometimes for longer stays. Although they were small, they still remember one long trek through the mountains to attend a Karen church convention at Musikee, which is a large area in the upper part of the Mae Chaem River drainage. We traveled together with the Dickerson family, who lived at Baw Gaow, the end of the road and jumping off place for treks into the surrounding mountains. It was a two day walk from Baw Gaow to Musikee, sleeping along the trail one night. However, we started on an afternoon, so we spent two nights along the trail. The Dickersons had brought rice and cooking pans, carried by two pack horses, so we ate rice and soup morning and evening. A Karen man traveling with us shot a squirrel one day, so we added that to the soup.

We stayed with a family in the Karen village of Mawta for four days. Our diet was mostly rice, with a few vegetables, so we were pleased to see a hunter come in one morning with a barking deer he had shot during the night. Barking deer are a small species of deer that do make a kind of barking noise. They are delicious.

Lani and Rebecca with the barking deer shot by a hunter.

After the convention we walked back to Baw Gaow, following the trail over the mountains and through the pine forests. At one place the trail skirted alongside a Hmong opium field. The opium had been harvested, but the dried stalks with their seed pods were still standing. We all stopped to crack open some of the pods and eat the poppy seeds. The drug is in the sap of green seed pods, none in the seeds. The children have never forgotten their trip to Musikee.

CHARLIE THE GOOSE

We raised geese in our yard when we lived in Chiang Rai. We ate some, gave some away, but they were most useful as guard animals. Whenever anyone entered our yard the geese would start to honk. At one time we had 19 geese. Nineteen geese a'honking is a lot of noise. When the geese started to honk our dog started to bark. It was really too much noise.

On Christmas Eve it is customary for young people from local churches to go caroling. They go from house to house all through the night, ending at dawn at a house that had been for-warned to feed them breakfast. Every house they visit also invites them in and provides candy, cookies or fruit. Our 19 geese honked at every group that came to our house. They were so loud they often drowned out the sweet sounds of the familiar carols. It was a bit much.

We reduced our flock to three adults; two females and one gander. Rebecca learned to keep her distance from the geese. One day, when a goose was sitting on a nest, she felt under it to count the eggs. The goose bit her on the arm, and Rebecca jerked her arm back, resulting in scratches from the serrated beak of the goose.

Our children named the gander Charlie. Charlie was a most unusual goose. He was very protective of his two wives, and, especially newly hatched goslings. No one could get near the goslings without being honked at, hissed at, and even chased.

You could be excused for thinking Charlie was mean. Charlie, however, had another side. When there were no goslings, and both females were sitting on their nests, Charlie got lonely. He would honk plaintively until Lani and Rebecca came out to play with him. He would sit on their laps and enjoy being petted. Never before, or since, have I seen a goose like Charlie.

Shortly before returning to the United States for a furlough in 1972 both of the female geese died. Charlie was distraught. Every day he circled our yard, honking loudly, looking for his mates who were not there. We invited some friends over for dinner a few days before our departure and it was my idea to serve Charlie to the guests. The kids started a "Save Charlie" protest, but I chopped his head off and we ate him. He was good, but Lani and Rebecca never ate a bite. I was a farmer's son. That's what we did with animals; we either ate them or sold them for someone else to eat. Sometimes fathers make mistakes. I should have found a home for Charlie while we were gone. The girls have never forgotten their friend, Charlie the goose.

Lani and Rebecca with Charlie the goose.

Family portrait, 1967.

MEETING THE PRINCESS MOTHER OF THAILAND

Princess Mother was the title given to the mother of His Majesty, The King Of Thailand. She was greatly loved and respected by all Thai people. Sometimes the Queen is thought of as being the Mother of the Nation, and so the Princess Mother was the Grandmother of the Nation. Actually, she was the mother of two kings. I don't believe that had ever happened before in Thai history. Her oldest son, His Majesty King Ananda Mahidiol, was crowned king in 1934. However, he was assassinated in the palace in 1946. That incident has never been fully explained and greatly shocked the nation. His younger brother was living the carefree life of a student in Switzerland, far from the formalities and expectations of royalty living in Thailand. However, upon the death of his brother he returned to his homeland and became king in 1946. His full name is His Majesty King Bhumibol Adulyadej, the Ninth Sovereign of the House of Chakri.

His mother is thus honored by being the mother of two kings. Her husband was of high royalty, but was not a king. After their marriage they lived in the United States for a few years where he studied medicine at Harvard Medical School. Her second son, the present king, was born in America during that time. After returning to Thailand she has spent very little time living in luxurious palaces, but traveled throughout the country visiting the common people and giving them aid in times of need. The Princess Mother died July 25th 1995 at age 95 and the entire nation went into mourning. To show love and respect a very elaborate cremation ceremony was arranged nearly a year after her death. Her body had been kept in an urn. A great mass of people came out to pay their last respects at the cremation ceremony in Bangkok. It lasted for hours. Dee and I watched on television from our home in Chiang Mai.

As we watched the ceremony my mind went back to 1971 when I had met the Princess Mother in a Tribal village. It all started when Thra David, the headman from the Karen village of Tung Praow, came to Sahasatsuksa School at Namlat Village near Chiang Rai with an urgent request. He said the Princess Mother was coming to his village the following week to open a Border Police school. Thra David wanted some of the students to come and sing for the Princess Mother. Some of the students were Karens and Lahus from in, or near, Tung Praow Village where the Border Police School was to be opened. The headman wanted some of those students, who had already received some education, to be there when the Princess Mother arrived.

For many years there had been virtually no schools in the mountain areas where the Hill Tribes lived, but in the 1970's the Thai Border Police were assigned the task of building simple classrooms and teaching elementary grades in some of the mountain villages. The Border Police were also there to provide law and order, suppress illegal drug production and provide protection against Communist insurgents. Most villagers did not like the regular police, whose behavior was not always good, but the Border Police did receive some special training in how to win the hearts and minds of the village people, and were better received. They also provided some basic medical care.

Khru Pipat, one of the teachers at Sahasatsuksa School, improvised a group of older Karen and Lahu students who came from the Tung Praow area, and also some local Karens, to be an orchestra, consisting of a violin, guitars, drum, and a homemade single- string bass. Two days later our group of about 15 left for Tung Praow, some in my Land Rover and some by a small local bus. We met up again in the District town of Mae Suey, where the foot trail to Tung Praow began. It was a four hour walk up into the mountains over the same trail that the Germans and I had led the cows to a Lahu village. Have you ever hiked to the accompaniment of a drum? It seemed that whoever was carrying the drum couldn't resist beating on it. Anyway, it did lift our spirits and seemed to make the hike easier. We arrived at the village after dark and divided up to sleep in different homes. The headman invited me to stay in his home.

The following day the students who were not from this village visited their own families in nearby villages. During the day Border Police and soldiers kept arriving in the village. They were to provide protection for the Princess Mother when she arrived by helicopter the following day. By late afternoon Tribal people were streaming in from the surrounding hills. They wanted to be sure to see the Princess Mother. They were dressed in their finest clothes. As in most cultures, it was the women who were the most ornately garbed. The Lahu women wore their black skirts with red stripes and an outer tunic trimmed with red and white appliqué. Silver ornaments decorated the upper part of the tunic and they wore heavy silver earrings.

The Akha women came in their black pleated knee length skirts, the shortest skirts of all the Tribal people. It rides low in the hips, but they are modestly covered by a hip length jacket. A sash, brightly decorated with beads and cowry shells, is tied around their waist. They wore leggings and the distinctive Akha headdress covered with silver ornaments and tassels of monkey fur dyed red.

The Lisu women were the most colorful of all in their blue knee-length pants with an outer tunic of blue or green split up the sides to the waist. The yoke of the tunic was made of black cloth to which bands of cloth in many bright colors had been attached. They wore a black sash more than 6 yards long wound around their waist. Attached to the sash in the back are two tassels, like tails, which sway back and forth as they walk. Their heads were adorned with black turbans to which long threads of colored yarn had been attached.

The Karen women came in two styles, depending on their marital status. Single girls wore plain white cotton shifts with a band of red at the waist and at the bottom of the garment. Married Karen women wore more colorful clothes, consisting of a woven red sarong with stripes of yellow and blue. They wore pullover blouses with a woven pattern, or with seeds sewed on in a geometric pattern. That day all the mountain trails led to Tung Praow Village as each ethnic group came dressed in their finest to see the Princess Mother.

That night they camped in family groups around the Border Police School, and the police organized an impromptu program of entertainment. The Karen orchestra played, and each group was asked to sing a song or perform a traditional dance. The stage was lit by the flickering light of bonfires. A modern Thai love song might be followed by a recitation of ancient Karen poetry, or an Akha dance. A young Karen man even sang some modern Western songs in English. Never have I heard "Your Cheating Heart" sung in such a setting!

The Thai Border Police had been sipping on Mae Khong whiskey and a little later in the program they thought it would be a good idea to teach the local maidens how to *ram wong*, which is a more modern type of Thai dance. Some of the Akha girls were coaxed up on the stage but they didn't know how to *ram wong*. The police gave a brief demonstration of the dance, which consists of stylized feet and hand movements but no body contact. The Karen orchestra started playing and away they went. The results were less than successful. However, the attempt did contribute to the general entertainment of the audience. I hoped the Border Police teachers would have better success in teaching the children how to read and write! The show wound down about midnight and we all retired to our sleeping places.

Khru Pipat was up early the next morning rehearsing his students and the orchestra in the song he had written to sing to the Princess Mother. It told how "We Hill Tribe people are loyal to Country and King." Three helicopters arrived in the morning with more soldiers, doctors and government officials. The doctors set up a clinic in the school building and conducted an out-patient clinic all day. His Majesty the King's sister, Her Royal Highness Princess Galyani Wattana, and two of her friends were on one of those helicopters. They walked up to the village where I met them. They wanted to know who I was and how I had got there. When I told them I had walked in with some young students who were going to school elsewhere, they were very interested and wanted to meet some of those students. I took them on a tour of the village and ended up at the headman's house. His daughter was one of the students I had brought. They talked with her and asked some questions about her life. The student didn't realize who she was talking to. The King's sister never did identify herself but I recognized her from seeing her picture in the newspapers.

At about 1:00 P.M. two more helicopters arrived with the Princess Mother and her entourage. The Border Policemen lined up everyone so the Princess Mother could walk between us as she went up to the school. She wore a military type uniform with trousers. A chair had been prepared for her with a parachute canopy over it for shade. I had about 500 pencils with me from the Rotary Club of Chiang Rai, of which I was a member. I had told one of the officials who was organizing things that I had those pencils and wanted to give them to the Princess Mother for the Border Police School. After the Princess Mother was seated my name was called out and I walked up with my bundle of pencils wrapped up in old paper.

I was dressed in the clothing of a Lahu man and must have been a puzzling sight. I'm sure she wondered what a blond-headed, round-eyed, big-nosed foreigner was doing there. I bowed before her and offered my gift of pencils.

"These pencils are a gift to this Border Police School from the Rotary Club of Chiang Rai.," I told her.

One of her aids took it from my hands and laid it beside her chair. She was quite curious about me and asked several questions.

"I'm surprised to see you," she said in very good English. "How did you get here?"

"I walked from the Mae Suey Market," I replied.

"That must be a very long walk."

"Not too bad, only about four hours."

"Do you come here often?"

"I have been here several times before."

"What do you do?"

"I am an agricultural missionary. I help these Tribal people improve their livelihood by teaching better farming methods."

"Oh, that is very good. They do need help. Did you come alone?"

"No, I came with some Tribal students from another school who would like to sing to you."

"They can do that after the ceremony to open the school. I will be looking for them."

"Oh, one more thing," she added. "Next week I will be on bivouac at the Payao Fish Hatchery. Do you know where that is?"

"Yes," I replied. "I often go there to get fish fingerlings to take to village fish ponds."

"I would like you and your wife to have dinner with me there. You will hear from the Chiang Rai Provincial Government Office about the arrangements." She gave me a medal with the King's emblem on it and I returned to our group of excited students who were waiting to sing. Now I was excited too. Dinner with the Princess Mother. Wow!

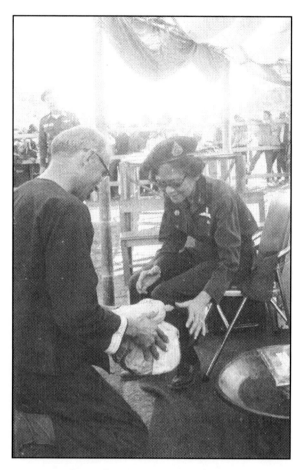

Rupert presenting school supplies to the Princess Mother.

When the school opening ceremony was finished she came out to see the people and gave gifts to all the children. When she came near our group the official with her in charge of arrangements signaled for us to start. The Karen orchestra started to play and Khru Pipat led the students in singing all four verses of the song he had written for the Princess Mother. She thanked us for the fine song and asked some more questions about the students. She proceeded on to her helicopter and departed in a cloud of dust.

Our students were really impressed. They would have something to talk about for the rest of their lives.

Some of our students who sang for the Princess Mother.

We also packed up and hit the trail to return to the town of Mae Suey where I had parked my Land Rover. It was late in the afternoon and people from a large Akha village, which was on the way back, invited us to spend the night in their village. I think they wanted to hear more from our musical group. People from that village helped carry our packs and the big drum. That was the same village where I had tied two cows to a post. I hoped they had forgiven me. It was dark before we arrived and somewhere on the trail ahead of us I could hear someone pounding on the big drum.

After arriving in this village of about 60 houses we were taken to the house we were to stay in. I suggested the girls stay inside the house with Khru Wanphen, one of the lady teachers from Sahasatsuksa School who had come with us. We fellows could sleep on the porch just outside. As I expected, the Karen orchestra now had to make music for the Akha until midnight.

We were in a house next to the Akha headman's house and the *Nai Amphur* (District Officer) of Mae Suey District was staying overnight with the headman. He also had been to the school opening. The headman's two wives prepared a meal for him and the District Officer invited me to eat with him. I asked him if the girl students and one lady teacher could eat with us also, as I had seen no evidence of food preparation in the house in which we were staying. He assured me that would be all right. We were served rice and about the toughest chicken I have ever chewed on in my life.

Later in the evening I walked down to the courting circle in the center of the village. This was a traditional Akha village, so large logs had been placed in a kind of circle where the young unmarried people could gather at night. Several couples were sitting on the logs, some of them hugging and kissing. It reminded me of the steps of a dormitory for women on an American college campus ten minutes before curfew. However, it was so surprising to see this in Southeast Asia. None of the other ethnic groups allow such intimacy between young unmarried men and women. I was glad the Karen lady teacher was not with me. She would have been totally shocked! There were five older married Akha women standing together. Maybe they were the chaperones. They were singing old Akha songs in a kind of chant. The leader of the group would hit a note and the rest would chime in. It was really great.

I went back to my assigned house about midnight to find the girl students and lady teacher still awake and sitting up in the house. They had heard false rumors about Akha morals and activities related to sex. There were several men sitting around in the same room talking, so the girls were afraid to stretch out and sleep on the floor mats provided for them. Akha houses are divided into a men's side and a women's side. We were in the men's side, which is also where guests stay. Eventually, things quieted down. The girls slept with all their clothing on inside the house, and we men slept out on the porch.

We were rudely awakened at 5:30 A.M. by the Akha women pounding rice under the porch. All the tribal people use a similar device to remove the outer husk from the rice grains before the rice can be cooked. It is basically a huge foot operated mortar and pestle, consisting of a heavy pole about 10 feet long balanced on an upright frame. At one end of the pole a smaller piece of wood is attached. That piece is rounded on one end and it is made to fall into a large block of wood with a hole in it. Unhulled rice is placed in that hole. One woman, or two small girls, step on the long pole at the other end raising up the pole. They release it and it falls with a heavy thud. The vertical piece of wood on the other end drops into the hole containing rice. After doing that many, many times the hulls are pounded off and the rice and hulls are scooped out by hand and put in a flat winnowing tray. When enough rice has been pounded it is winnowed to separate out three separate items; the rice to eat, rice bran to feed pigs and the outer hulls which are discarded. That morning an Akha girl about eight years old was expertly doing the winnowing by flipping the winnowing tray up and down. The rice grains accumulated on one side of the tray, and the lighter chaff on the other side. It looked easy, so I asked if I could try. I just mixed everything up and nothing got separated. The little girl thought it was funny and covered her mouth to hide her giggles.

We soon gathered up our back packs and started down the trail to Mae Suey town. On the way we met some Thai people coming up to sell dogs to the Akha. The Akha eat dogs. We kidded one another about what that really was we had eaten the night before, and decided that tough chicken wasn't so bad after all. We arrived in Mae Suey town about 10:00 A.M., reclaimed my Land Rover from where I had parked it and drove back to the school to drop off the students and teachers. When I got home Dee asked me what had happened up there in the hills during the last three days. I replied that I had tried to winnow rice but couldn't do it. She laughed at me too. She was really impressed, however, when I told her that we were invited to eat with the Princess Mother. "But I don't have a thing to wear," she wailed.

DINING WITH ROYALTY

A few days after the opening of the Border Police School I received a note from the office of the Governor of Chiang Rai Province informing me that Her Highness, The Queen Mother, had invited Mrs. Nelson and me to dine with her at the Fish Hatchery in Payao, a district town about 100 kilometers south of Chiang Rai, on the evening of February 8, 2514. In the Buddhist Era calendar used in Thailand, the year 2514 corresponded with the year 1971 in the Western calendar. The note further stated that the Queen Mother would arrive by helicopter at 2:00 P.M. and stay at the Fish Hatchery for 3 days.

I knew the Fish Hatchery well as I had often driven there to pick up fish fingerlings to use in stocking village fish ponds. It was not a large place and had only a few wooden buildings, consisting of an office and staff housing, in addition to the tanks used to propagate and hold the fingerlings. I presumed that was why the Princess Mother had told me in the village that she would be "bivouacking" there.

Dee spoke to several of her Thai friends to find out what she should wear for the occasion. The consensus was that she should wear a Thai outfit, consisting of a long, sarong type skirt with matching blouse made from Thai silk in the style that Thai women wear on formal occasions. I'm sure it would have been quite acceptable for a foreigner to wear western clothe, but since Dee is Chinese-American, and could pass as Thai, her friends thought she should wear formal Thai dress. Dee had already had such a dress made and it hung in her closet, so she, indeed, did have something to wear. I would wear a suit and tie. No problem.

On the appointed day, Dee and I and our seven year old daughter, Rebecca, drove to Payao. Our older daughter, Lani, was attending a boarding school in Chiang Mai. The Thai military helicopter landed in an open field near the Fish Hatchery. Thai government officials, plus the three of us, lined up to greet the Princess Mother. She remembered me as she passed by and paused to say she was glad I was there. Her American friend, Miss Betty Dumaine, was with her. They had become friends many years before when the Princess Mother was living in Boston with her husband while he attended Harvard Medical School. One of the palace aids with her reminded us that dinner would be at 7:30 P.M.

We spent the rest of the afternoon with Reverend and Mrs. Laufer, who were German missionaries living in Payao. Rebecca stayed with them when Dee and I returned to the Fish Hatchery that evening. Tables had been set up in an open area under one of the wooden buildings. The Princess Mother was staying in a room upstairs. A number of high government officials were there dressed in their formal civil service uniforms. Drinks were served while we waited. Soon the Princess Mother descended the stairs and one of her attendants advised us that we should *fao* Her Highness. That meant we should come into her presence. There followed a somewhat awkward moment as no one seemed to know what to do, or say. Thai people are always somewhat awed in the presence of their royalty and prefer to remain silent rather than say something foolish. The Princess Mother, however, was a good mixer and moved from person to person making small talk and making everyone feel at ease. She was dressed very informally in black slacks, a European peasant blouse, low shoes and white socks.

Dee and I were conversing with Betty Dumaine and The Queen Mother came and joined us.

"Mr. Nelson, tell me more about the students who sang for me in the village. Were they really Hill Tribe children?"

"Yes," I replied. They were Karen and Lahu. One of the teachers with me was also a Karen."

"That's wonderful. How did that school get started?"

I told her the school had been started by American missionaries to provide an education for Hill Tribe children. I mentioned I had an advisory role at the school, but most of my work was agricultural development in Tribal villages. I even told her about the 4-H Club we had recently organized at the school. Thailand does have an Agricultural Extension Service and 4-H clubs patterned after the American system. She thought that was really great and decided to give me some garden seeds for the 4-H Club members. She immediately got up and went to another building to get the seeds for me.

There were six small tables, each set for four people, and a larger table set for six. When it was time to eat I was surprised to be invited to eat at the larger table with the Princess Mother. Also at that table was Betty Dumaine, the vice governor of the province, the provincial chief of police and another man I did not get acquainted with. We were served in courses: A Thai hot soup, steak with asparagus, fish, rice and peas, and a Thai dessert of sweetened green mung beans. The food was good, but most of the people at the table were somewhat ill at ease and tried to act very formal.

Dee sat at a table with Princess Momchowying Rangsit, and Khun Prida and his wife. Khun Prida was head of the Fisheries Department of the Thai government, and since the Princess Mother was staying at a Fish Hatchery under his supervision protocol demanded that he be present to act as host. Dee told them I often got fish fingerlings from this place to take to

Tribal villages. Later, Khun Prida told the administrator of the fish hatchery that from now on Mr. Nelson could get all the fingerlings he wanted at no cost.

The party broke up soon after dessert and Dee and I returned to the Laufer residence to pick up Rebecca. We drove on back to our home in Chiang Rai late at night in our old pickup model Land Rover. The ball was over. We were back in our pumpkin!

Eating dinner with the Princess Mother; L to R, Police Chief of Chiang Rai Province, Betty Dumaine, Vice Governor, Rupert, government official, Princess Mother.

UP COUNTRY RUMORS

In 1973, after a furlough spent in Bozeman, Montana, our family moved from Chiang Rai to Chiang Mai, which was a larger city to the south of us, but still in northern Thailand. It was a more central location for the Karen population of Thailand, and there were some other advantages. In Chiang Mai there was an English speaking school for foreign children. Dee would not have to home school Lani and Rebecca anymore.

After moving to northern Thailand, we had found the information dissemination system to be quite different from Bangkok. This was just as true in the Chiang Mai area as it had been in Chiang Rai. People were less sophisticated, less literate, and perhaps less inclined to believe the newspapers, which were printed in Bangkok. Much information was spread by word of mouth, and perhaps to engender a little excitement, those repeating information would often embellish on the facts considerably. Rumors were always circulating about minor affairs and people did not take them too seriously.

In small village life everybody knows everything about everybody else in the village. Political events and personalities in far off Bangkok are of little or no concern to rural villagers in Chiang Rai or Chiang Mai Provinces. We did find, however, that occasionally rumors of a very serious nature would sweep through an entire area, or even the entire country. Bangkok, with its urban sophistication, usually was not affected. These were rumors for the country people.

The first such rumor to come to our attention was about the "blood taking people." That rumor created great anxiety and people were afraid to travel alone for fear of being caught by the "blood takers." During a period of nearly a year, it was generally believed all through northern Thailand that there were people going around taking blood by force. If they caught someone alone, they would withdraw that person's blood into a large syringe: all his blood. Some versions of the rumor said the blood was for Communist terrorists hiding in the hills who needed the blood for their wounded comrades. Other versions said the blood was taken to be sold. Everywhere you went there was someone who knew of a person in the next village who was found dead with a needle mark on him and his blood removed. One morning the Chiang Mai Market was buzzing with excited talk when I went to buy fruit.

"What's wrong this morning?" I asked the fruit vendor.

"Haven't you heard? The blood takers got another one right here in the market."

"Right here in town? When?"

"Just a little while ago. A man and wife were selling vegetables and left their child sleeping in the back of their pickup. When they came back, their child was dead."

"Wow, that's close to home. But how do you know it was the blood takers?"

"Oh, it was, it was. Everybody knows it was."

The local newspapers, quick to report on sensational happenings, reported many alleged instances of blood taking and even reported that the police caught a blood taker and took him off to jail. It always seemed to happen to someone else, and the reports were second hand. I never talked to anyone who actually had seen it happen, or even seen the corpse. The important fact was, however, that everyone believed it was happening.

One day during that period, Moody Taw, a Lahu man, and I went to a Lahu village about 100 kilometers north of Chiang Mai. I drove in my Land Rover. The trail into the village was seldom used by vehicles and was overgrown badly with grass and brush. After repairing a bridge, we drove on into the village, only to receive an odd welcome. Not many motorized vehicles arrived in that village, so ordinarily people would gather around to see the strange sight. That day, however, we only caught glimpses of women as they scurried to their houses herding their children with them. Some of the women reappeared at the doorway of their homes holding machetes in their hands.

They recognized Moody and me when we stepped out of the Land Rover and suddenly everyone gathered around laughing and talking, evidently in great relief. I didn't understand Lahu, so I had to wait until Moody found out what was going on so he could tell me. Moody explained that there had been reports of blood takers in the area, and, supposedly, they were traveling in a Land Rover. Just the day before, a man in a neighboring village was found dead, a victim of the blood takers. On the day we had arrived most of the men in the village were out working in their fields, so the arrival of my Land Rover threw the women into a panic. They weren't cowed, however, and stood ready to defend their children with machetes in hand.

Eventually the blood taking rumors died away. Whether or not there was any basis of truth in the rumors I'll never know. I have been told that the collection and preservation of fresh blood under field conditions would be almost impossible. Whether true or not, it certainly was widely believed to be true throughout all of northern Thailand.

That rumor was followed by another widespread belief which provided some light relief for some of us, but certainly was considered to be very serious by the male portion of the population. I believe that rumor started in Northeast Thailand, but rapidly spread to the northern part of the country. It was believed there were people going around injecting a chemical substance in food products. If that food was eaten by a man, his penis would shrink back up into his body. Understandably, the men were concerned even more about that rumor than they had been about the blood takers! The malady was known as the "shrinking disease."

There were different stories as to who was responsible and why. The most common explanation was that the Communists were doing this to stir up dissension in the country. If anything bad was going on, either the Communists or the CIA was blamed for it. There supposedly were some ingenious methods of injecting food products, such as the person who carried a concealed syringe in his hand connected to a hose extending on up to his armpit where the hose enlarged to a round ball. When the person squeezed his arm down on the ball, the liquid drug would squirt out of the concealed syringe into fresh food in the markets.

Oranges were considered to be choice targets. A friend of mine was once traveling with some Lahus. He bought a bag of oranges in a market to eat along the way, but no one would eat them. Cigarettes were also suspected and that created a real dilemma for smokers; whether to give up smoking or take the risk of losing their manhood. Some brands, reportedly, were more suspect than others. A Thai newspaper even printed an article comparing all the brands sold in Thailand in order of the incidence of the malady supposedly caught from them.

Doctors were swamped with worried men patients who claimed their organ began to shrink soon after eating some food or smoking a cigarette. Men would even come to a clinic holding on tight to their organ to prevent its disappearance.

During this period, Paul Dodge, a Baptist missionary, and Wallace Paw Yo, a Lahu from Chiang Mai, went with me to a Lahu village in Chiang Rai province. We went to meet with villagers about the possibilities of establishing a training center and agricultural demonstration farm near that village. Again, we went in my Land Rover. There was supposed to be a road off the main highway part way to the Lahu village, but it turned out to be nonexistent. There was a foot path and ox carts had been over the trail, so I put the Land Rover in low range 4-wheel drive and took off through streams, over rocks, and through tall grass. Ox carts have a high clearance from the ground, so there was always the danger of stumps or rocks hidden in the grass. Much of the way Paul Dodge walked in front of the Land Rover looking for such obstructions.

The road ended at a Lisu village located on the banks of the Mae Lao River, and there we parked our Land Rover. We had also brought two young boar pigs with us for breeding purposes. One was for the Lahu village, but one was for Namlat village near Chiang Rai. We had arranged to meet someone from that village here, but they did not arrive. The pigs were in covered baskets so we left them in the Land Rover. If necessary, we could send someone back for the one that belonged in the Lahu village.

We had to cross the Mae Lao River, and it was running high from heavy rains. There was no bridge, but there was a primitive ferry operated with a heavy wire strung across the river. Attached to this wire by ropes were two small bamboo rafts, both of which were on the far side. There were some Lahu boys swimming on that side so Wallace yelled at them to bring a ferry across. This they did, though somewhat reluctantly. It was no easy task. The current was swift, so the rope from the boat to the wire was stretched tight. The boys had to stand on the raft and slide the rope along the wire, moving about two feet at a time. There were numerous splices in the wire which delayed things even more. Finally, the raft arrived. It was small, so when we all climbed on, it nearly sank. Wallace was frightened and said he would wait and go on the second trip. Paul and I went across slowly. The raft was about six inches below water the entire trip, so we couldn't sit down. We sort of semi-squatted with our bed rolls on our backs to keep them dry. That was the most uncomfortable ferry ride I ever had. After we arrived on the far bank, the boys went back again for Wallace. He came across in similar fashion, hanging on for dear life.

Relieved to have the river behind us, we continued on foot for about thirty minutes to the Lahu village. We planned to spend the night there and go on to Chiang Rai the following day. Together with some villagers, we looked over the proposed training center site. It really was a nice location. Some lowlands could be made into rice paddies using a small stream for irrigation water. There was a pond, and some higher land on which to build classroom and training buildings. After looking around until nearly dark, we returned to the house where we were to stay and found dinner waiting. A low, carved wooden table was heaped high with steaming rice. Enameled bowls held curries made from pork, and small bamboo containers held the fiery chili pepper sauce which the Lahus dearly love.

After we had eaten, the women cleared the remaining food away and served tea. Men and women from all the houses in the village now started arriving until the house was packed and I feared for the bamboo floor. Wallace explained our purpose of looking for a site for a Lahu agricultural training center. The villagers were eager to have it built in their village, and offered suggestions on how to clear the land and acquire legal title. The details began to get a bit tedious and I wished the meeting would end so I could crawl into my sleeping bag.

About 9:00 P.M. a man appeared at the door and started speaking to those nearest him. Soon everyone in the room was listening to him. The conversation was in Lahu, so I asked Wallace what the problem was.

"His son has the shrinking disease," Wallace replied, "and he wants you to take him to the hospital in Chiang Rai." Visions of crossing the river in the dark and driving back out on the nonexistent road flashed through my mind.

"No, that is impossible," I said. "We will go in the morning."

167

The boy's father now began to speak to Paul and me in the Northern Thai dialect urging us to take his son to the hospital tonight before it was too late. Our meeting wasn't over yet and I had no intention of leaving until morning, so I gave the man two aspirin to give to his son and told him to tell his son to lie down and relax.

The man went out and we proceeded with our meeting. It wasn't to last. Soon there was another discussion at the doorway, and Wallace said the young man himself was there. Someone suggested that if I wasn't convinced of the young man's problem, I should examine him myself. I certainly wasn't convinced, so I took a flashlight and the young man and went into a bedroom of the house. I made my inspection and everything looked normal to me, except the poor fellow was holding on to his organ to prevent it from shrinking away up inside his abdomen. I went back into the main room and made an announcement to everyone there, which was most of the village. I said, "Everything is fine, nothing is disappearing, and if this young many would just lie down and relax everything would go away."

"Go away" really was a poor choice of words in that situation! Another long discussion followed in Lahu. I assumed they were discussing the matter, so I just sat back and relaxed. It may seem odd to Westerners that a subject of a somewhat delicate nature would be so openly debated, with men and women both taking part. Village life is a very face-to-face society and there are few secrets. I'm afraid someone who valued privacy would have a hard time of it in a small Asian village. If you are a part of a village, however, you also receive the support of the community. Everyone was concerned about the welfare of the young man and debating the best course of action.

Apparently my medical diagnosis was not acceptable. Wallace informed me that the consensus was that the fellow should go to the hospital, and, since I had the only vehicle, I should take him. Sometimes all one can do is bow to the inevitable. The village had come to a consensus of what course of action to take. I could have refused, but that would have been considered boorish and cruel behavior.

With a sigh, I began to pack up my backpack, as did Paul and Wallace. Then I remembered the pig. The men who had gone back to the Land Rover to get the pig had brought both pigs back to the village. One of those was going to the village near Chiang Rai, so it had to go back with us. Wallace recruited two men to carry the pig in a basket with a carrying pole, and our procession straggled out of the village at about 10:00 P.M. There was no moon and it was incredibly dark. The two or three flashlights in our group were not very effective as we stumbled back over the ill defined trail, tripping over stumps and occasionally wandering off in wrong directions. Finally, we came to the banks of the river, and, fortunately, one ferry boat was on our side. The Lahu villagers who had carried the pig took charge of the ferry. It took three laborious trips to get us all across the river. Again the ferry "floated" six inches below the surface as we squatted uncomfortably, holding backpack and shoes. About halfway across, my flashlight slipped out of my pocket and into the rushing water. No use trying to retrieve it. It was gone.

We struggled up the far bank and on to the Land Rover. About six people, including the patient and his parents, crawled into the back of the Land Rover, together with the protesting pig. Paul, Wallace, and I sat in front.

Up ahead, in the center of the Lisu village was a large bonfire. Only when I had driven up to it did we realize it was right in the middle of the road. It turned out to be a Lisu courting circle. Young men and women were sitting around the fire, boys on one side and girls on the other. When we arrived, they were improvising courting songs. Wallace understands Lisu so he could explain what they were singing. A boy would sing a verse or two with the words aimed at one of the girls. The double meanings and suggestive lyrics would cause peals of laughter from both the boy's and girl's sides of the fire. When the boy finished, the girl would answer through her song. Her answer would be a kind of a rebuff, but still leaving the door open for further negotiations. Those songs were made up as they went along and required fast thinking and good use of words to get the proper shade of meaning across. Sometimes a boy would play on a Lisu flute made from bamboo.

We sat watching on the outer edge of the circle, fascinated by what was taking place before our eyes. A custom as old as mankind, whereby two people find themselves drawn to one another, make a commitment to live together in a manner sanctioned by their society, and begin a family, repeating the process over again.

Reluctantly, we asked them to move the fire so we could proceed. The road had not improved any and sometimes we lost it entirely. At one time I got hung up on a stump and all the passengers, except the patient and the pig, had to get out and rock the Land Rover off the stump. The main highway to Chiang Rai was a most welcome sight. After reaching it, we were able to speed on into the town, arriving at the hospital at midnight.

A hospital orderly met us. "What's wrong?" he inquired. "I have a man with the shrinking disease," I replied, not knowing what his reaction would be. He accepted this information just as if I had said our patient had a broken arm. Our passengers disembarked with the patient to comfort him in his time of need. Typically, doctors treated this malady with a mild sedative or a placebo, and the patient, reassured, soon was healed.

The three of us drove on out to the village of Namlat where we knew people. That also was the pig's destination. Namlat is primarily a Karen and Thai village, but two Lahu families also lived there. We arrived at their houses at 1:00 a.m. Upon identifying ourselves to the sleepy voices inside, we were invited in and provided with sleeping places, which we gratefully used for the balance of the night.

As we were driving back to Chiang Mai the following day, Paul and I discussed the previous night's events and how hard it would be to try to explain it to a Western audience. Paul is from Maine, and has the dry sense of humor typical of his tribe. His final comment was that if anyone asked how the patient was doing, we could always reply, "Well, he's still holding his own!"

CHANGING ATTITUDES

After we had become involved in our work in northern Thailand among the upland Tribal people occasional visitors would find their way to our door asking if I would mind taking them to see the Hill Tribes or if Mrs. Nelson would help them go shopping. Usually, we would be too busy to oblige, but some visitors were more in the line of duty and required our attention.

As I observed those Americans, or other Westerners, I began to realize how much my own attitudes were changing. Thailand was changing me. I saw how true that was one time when I received a visit from a man representing a charitable organization that had provided a grant to start a cattle raising project among the Lahu people.

Shortly after the project started an executive in that organization, whom I will call Richard, wrote to announce that he was coming to inspect the project. He wrote that he would stay in Bangkok and devote one day to visit the Lahu Cattle Project. I hurriedly responded and informed him that Chiang Mai was a long way from Bangkok and that the village where the project was located was a day's journey from Chiang Mai. He was able to adjust his schedule and arrived in Chiang Mai by plane late one afternoon. I took him to the Chiang Inn Hotel and told him I would pick him up the following morning at 6:00 A.M. He appeared anxious to complete this trip and get back to Bangkok where he had some business with the Thai Government Livestock Department. Richard was not pleased when I told him it would not be possible to visit the cattle project and return to Chiang Mai in one day. We would have to spend one night in the Lahu village.

I was beginning to notice that Americans were always in a hurry. They filled every moment with activities. They stressed that time is money. Time is critical. Time is running out. Rural Thailand sets a slower pace. The people follow an agricultural cycle of rice planting and harvesting. Time is seen as being cyclical, not a straight line with a beginning and an ending. Thais always have time for *sanuk* (fun). Richard was an American in a hurry.

When I arrived at the hotel in my Land Rover promptly at 6:00 A.M. I was rather dismayed to see Richard dressed in a good pair of slacks, sport shirt, street shoes and carrying a nice leather suitcase. I suggested some more appropriate clothes for traveling in the jungle, but he said that was all he had.

First, we drove to Fang, about 180 kilometers north of Chiang Mai. Wallace Paw Yo, a Lahu man from Chiang Mai, accompanied us. Wallace was with me when we encountered the young man with the shrinking disease. He was also involved in helping set up this livestock raising project among his people. He had previously lived in Burma and spoke English. At Fang we stopped in the market and had a lunch of rice and curry, but soon proceeded on to the small town of Ta Tawn, located on the bank of the Mae Kok River near the Burma border. There we parked the Land Rover in an enclosed compound belonging to a local merchant.

Richard was delighted when he heard we would now take a boat for the next portion of our journey, that is, until he saw the boat. It was a typical Thai river boat which I had often ridden without any serious accidents. Well, one time we did sink and I lost two cameras and a shoulder bag. There was another time on the River Kwai when a boat coming fast around a bend rammed the one Dee and me and our two children were in and injured our boatman, but there really was no use in bothering Richard with such details.

Our boat was long and narrow, made from a hollowed out log with sideboards tacked on the sides to increase the headboard. There were no seats, just mats on the bottom of the boat. Perhaps more important, there was no roof to protect us from the hot noon sun. A Wisconsin air cooled engine was in the rear of the boat with a long shaft extending ten feet from the rear into the water. The propeller was at the end of this maneuverable shaft with which the boat was controlled. Those types of boats are called *hangyao* (long tailed) boats.

We boarded the boat and piled Wallace's and my back packs as well as Richard's suitcase in the front of the boat. The boat felt rather tippy and Richard commented that he sure was glad there were only the three of us, plus the boatman. I didn't have the heart to tell him what I knew was coming. The boatman had told Wallace and me that a few people were waiting to go down the river too, and this was the only boat available that day. I've never known a boat to go unless filled above capacity, so I accept the inevitable.

Richard got noticeably nervous when three more people got into the boat, protested severely when five more arrived, and got somewhat hysterical when four more people arrived with two large bags of rice, a basket of chickens, a small pig, various cooking pots and a large saw.

The boatman eased us out into the main current of the river. No one dared move much, especially Richard, as there was only about one inch of freeboard from the surface of the water to the top of the boat. Water seeped in, as usual, along the crack where the sideboards were tacked on to the hollowed out log. I knew that when it got deep enough someone would start bailing with a tin can. Since the engine noise made it impossible to give Richard this information he just sat there rigid as a post.

I recognized another American trait in Richard that I was beginning to lose. My countrymen have a very well developed sense of property rights. "We paid to hire this boat," Richard had exclaimed earlier, "how come all these other people are getting in?" Some of the extra people were likely relatives of the boat owner. Others were friends who lived along the river. In Thai society it's impolite to say no. As long as there was space in the boat the boatman was obliged to take in those people, whom he knew well.

After going downstream for about an hour Wallace signaled the boatman to let us off on the right-hand bank. We disembarked, seeing no sign of human habitation. The expensive leather suitcase looked very strange sitting there in the elephant grass along the Mae Kok River. It did not blend into the environment. Wallace and I were using some old back packs. Richard looked around in bewilderment.

"Where are the cattle?" he asked.

"Oh, we have to walk a few hours to the Lahu village. That's where the cattle are located."

"Why are they so far away?"

No good answer came to mind, so I just said, "We'd better get moving." Wallace led the way on a trail that led away from the river, heading toward some distant hills. It didn't take long before both Wallace and I noticed that Richard was in trouble. His suitcase was obviously heavy, and he kept switching it from hand to hand, and his shirt was soaked with perspiration. Soon the trail skirted the edge of a Red Lahu village and Wallace led us up into the village and said he would find someone to carry the suitcase. Richard protested, but Wallace and I insisted that a carrier would be a good idea.

"You Foreigners sure have a lot of stuff," was a comment I often heard from Thai people. Carrying all your own "stuff" provides good motivation for traveling light. I had to admit I kept a lot of things at home, more than needed, but on trips like this I had learned to travel light. My backpack contained one change of clothe, a towel, light sleeping bag, a *pakama* (loin cloth), a bar of soap, toothpaste and a toothbrush. Americans do have a lot of "stuff", and tend to carry it around with them.

Just as we arrived in that small village of eight houses, some of the men were returning from a two day hunting trip. They were a tough looking bunch with their long hair and tattered pants with an international collection of rifles, shotguns, muzzle loaders, knives and bandoleers of cartridges slung over their bare torsos. They appeared angry, and, as a matter of fact, they were angry because their hunt had been unsuccessful. Richard began to look as if he would rather be on a sinking boat in the River! Wallace spoke to the men in the Lahu language, and one of them suddenly began to yell. Soon a woman, whom I presumed to be his wife, appeared out of one of the houses. He gave her his weapon, an old English army rifle, and took the suitcase from Richard's trembling hand. Again the Lahu began to yell and his wife returned to the house and came back with strips of bark to be used as rope. The man tied the bark around the suitcase and slung it on his back. The fancy suitcase looked as strange there as it had on the river bank. "I have hired this man to carry the suitcase for 20 baht ($1.00)," explained Wallace. The man had been hunting for two days and now started out with the suitcase on his back without resting or eating.

We followed the trail up into the hills, and Richard seemed glad to have the carrier. The trail crossed several small streams. Wallace and I, wearing canvas tennis shoes, just waded across. Richard, however, had to stop and remove shoes and socks, roll up trouser legs and wade gingerly across, bruising his tender feet on the rocks. On the opposite bank the procedure was reversed. Our progress was rather slow, but that allowed us to really see the country we were passing through. The hills were forested with teak trees, two species of oak, many other kinds of trees and giant bamboo. Those provided some shade and the going was somewhat cooler. Flocks of small parrots scolded us from the tree tops. At one point Wallace, who was in the lead, stopped and pointed to a circular symbol of woven bamboo placed along the trail. "Be careful," he said, "this is a warning of some kind." He looked around and soon spotted a crossbow, fully drawn, with an arrow in it ready to go. A cord from the crossbow was strung across a game trail. It was a kind of deadfall. A passing animal, such as a barking deer or wild pig, would hit the cord and release the arrow. The hunter took no responsibility for passing pedestrians. They were supposed to be able to read the sign! We continued on and darkness was nearly upon us when we reached our destination, the Lahu village of Wang Din.

Richard took one horrified look at the cluster of twenty houses made of bamboo with grass thatch roofs and insisted on returning to Chiang Mai. I explained to him that it was not possible to return at this time of day, and furthermore, I reminded him, he hadn't seen the cattle yet which was the sole purpose of the trip. On the edge of the village, near our path, was the bamboo corral for the cattle Richard had traveled so far to see. They were the local Zebu breed of cattle, and Richard was not impressed.

"These cows are too small," complained Richard, "you should have some Holsteins here. They really produce a lot of milk."

"People around here don't drink milk," I replied. "No market for it either."

Richard was surprised, "What do you mean they don't drink milk? What do the children eat?"

"Their mother's milk, until they're about two years old and after that rice, chili peppers and vegetables like everybody else."

Richard seemed to find that bit of news incomprehensible. "What do they do with their cows then?"

"They will sell them to cattle buyers who sell the meat in the markets around here."

"Oh! What you want are beef cattle, like Herefords or Angus. Not much meat on these animals."

"They are rather small," I conceded, "but they can live here. The breeds you mentioned are not adapted to this climate. They would die in a few months from the heat and ticks."

I knew that to be true. I had seen what happened to imported Western breeds of cattle in other places in Thailand. They could survive only with great expense of housing, feed and medicine. That was not possible in Wang Din. Richard, like many Americans, had fond memories of fat cattle grazing in green pastures producing great quantities of milk to feed children. A nice thought, but the realities of life in a Southeast Asian village are quite different.

The cattle raising venture in that village was a cooperative effort. They were owned by all the families in the village. One man had been selected by the villagers to care for the cattle and he came out to meet us. We were invited to stay in his house. It was a typical Lahu house built up off the ground and supported on wooden posts. It had a grass thatch roof and the walls and floor were made of split bamboo. The floors of such houses are rather flexible and sag a bit when walked on, causing one to feel as if he could break through. They are strong and resilient, but a large foreign lady of my acquaintance did actually break through the floor of such a house. The house was not elevated very high, so she was left standing on the ground under the house with her head still inside. She had landed on a pig sleeping peacefully in the shade under the house which squealed loudly. The antics of Foreigners do provide for some humor in an otherwise quiet existence!

Those bamboo floors are really very versatile. Not only are they made from a readily available local material, but they are not tightly woven together. This allows for some air movement through them and has a cooling effect. Besides, when sweeping the floor the housewife can just sweep to an especially large crack and let the dust fall through. Such cracks are especially convenient for betal nut chewers. That habit produces a lot of red saliva causing the chewer to spit often. Their aim is not always accurate, so the edges of favorite cracks are always stained a dark red.

We stooped through the low doorway and into the main living room of the house. Two small children were sleeping in a corner. In the center of the room was the fireplace, an earth-filled box on which our host lit a fire to boil water for tea. The smoke just went up through the grass roof.

Our luggage was placed against one of the walls and a reed mat placed on the floor for us to sit on. The carrier from the other village was given his pay and he immediately left to return to his home. Our host removed some unidentifiable meat drying on a rack over the fire and gave it to his wife. I assumed that was our dinner. The water in the soot-blackened tea kettle soon came to a boil and next came a kind of tea ceremony I have observed many times, although I'm sure it would never qualify as an art form, Richard watched in great fascination. Our host had placed three rather grimy glasses on a metal tray on the floor in front of him. He poured hot tea into one glass, rubbed his thumb quickly around inside the glass, swirled the tea around and poured it into the second glass. This was poured into the third glass, repeating the procedure with the thumb each time. After the final glass was thus made clean and suitable for his guests, he poured out this discarded hot tea, refilled each glass from the teapot and graciously handed a glass to each of us. It was a charming procedure, but I'm afraid it would not be acceptable at the Women's Garden Club in my old home town. Wallace and I enjoyed our tea, but Richard did not touch his.

Westerners are very concerned about cleanliness. "Cleanliness is next to Godliness." "Don't touch that, it's dirty," we tell our children. "Can we drink the water?" adult travelers ask one another. I subscribe to the germ theory, and I do take reasonable precautions in what I eat and drink, but politeness and sensitivity in a social situation are also important. Our host had cleaned the glasses in a time honored method. He was being thoughtful for our well being. Not to drink any of his tea could be seen as an insult, and besides, I was thirsty.

It had been a long and hot day so Wallace and I decided to take a bath in a nearby stream. We invited Richard to join us. He declined, but said he would come along for the walk. It was bath time for the village. Men, women and children were bathing in the stream. Following local custom, women bathe downstream from men. They wear a sarong while bathing and when they have completed their bath they slip into a dry one as the remove the wet one. A bit tricky, my wife says, but practice helps. Wallace and I used our *pakamas* wrapped around our hips and modestly removed our trousers before stepping into the water. In Southeast Asia, even groups of men only, or women only, do not strip naked in front of one another. The water was cool and very refreshing. After bathing, the women filled hollow sections of bamboo to carry back to their homes for household use.

Dinner was served shortly after we got back to the house. We sat on the floor around a low table. The meat turned out to be from a large lizard about three feet long called a *laen*. I had eaten this forest creature before and found it very good. The taste is like something halfway between chicken and fish. Cracked corn was mixed with the steamed rice because the village had experienced a poor rice crop and were short of their staple food. Since that was considered poor fare, our host apologized profusely for this low quality rice. I thought it was rather tasty myself.

Richard again refused tea, but ate with a hearty appetite, until he asked what the delicious meat was. I was afraid that question was coming, so I was prepared with an evasive answer. However, Wallace took it upon himself to describe in great detail the salient features of that particular species of lizard. Richard paled and didn't eat any more. I have observed that food likes and dislikes are all in the head.   Food high in protein is often in low supply in tribal villages, so all possible sources are exploited. Some of those food sources may seem strange to Americans, but prove to be very tasty when they get through the barrier of our own prejudices. Some of our Western food is likewise rejected by people in Thailand. Cheese is seen as simply awful.

We were in a Christian village, and apparently our host was the church choir leader. In the evening the house filled with men and women who came to choir practice. The three of us were crowded into a corner of the room and listened to the choir singing beautifully and with obvious pleasure. They sang in four part harmony and were really a joy to hear. Richard was thrilled and said he had never expected to hear anything like that. Music does uplift hearts around the world.

About 10:00 P.M. the choir left and we prepared for bed. The reed mats were again placed on the floor for us. I had also brought a sleeping bag for Richard, so we crawled into our bags. Wallace used a blanket.

"Why are you using a blanket and not a sleeping bag?" Richard asked Wallace.

"I never use a sleeping bag," replied Wallace, "it takes too long to get out of them if robbers or Communist terrorists come."

"Why wasn't I told of this," demanded Richard as he sat bolt upright.

"You're safer here than in most American cities," I assured him. "Anyway there are hardly any Communist terrorists in this area."

It is natural to feel vulnerable in places we have never been before, where the customs are different and where we don't understand the language. There were some Communist insurgents around at that time, but the only ones they bothered were Thai government people. I was able to communicate with the villagers and took my cue from the local people. They knew what was going on around them. Richard spent a restless night. I felt the floor moving from time to time as he twisted and turned around in his sleeping bag.

In the morning, before breakfast, we inspected the corrals and cattle more closely. The villagers told of their desire to raise cattle and of their hopes for this project. Its purpose was to start a foundation herd where Lahu villagers could obtain cattle cheaper than from the Thai cattle markets. It would be a continuing source of income for them. Basically, it was a good idea, and our visitor seemed convinced, although he still spoke wistfully of Holstein cows and clover pastures.

We returned to the house to eat breakfast. It was rice of course. Rice is served at every meal. We did have an egg omelet with it, which was very good and Richard ate well. We then retraced our trip of the previous day. One of the men from Wang Din village carried Richard's suitcase back to the banks of the Mae Kok River. We had to wait at the river bank until a boat came along that would stop to pick us up and bring us back to the boat landing at Tha Tawn. When we arrived there, Wallace went to look up an acquaintance while Richard and I reclaimed my Land Rover from the merchant's compound. Richard was having trouble speaking. His throat was dry.

"Do you suppose you could find me a bottle of beer in this place," he croaked.

It occurred to me that he had not drunk anything on that whole trip. Perhaps he was hesitant to make such a request of a missionary, but need overcame his reluctance. I took him to a restaurant and bought him a one liter bottle of Singha Thai beer. He took a long drink, looked at me and said, "You've just saved my life." Such gratitude I hadn't seen in a long time!

Later, when I was seeing him off at the Chiang Mai airport, he had taken a bath, cleaned his shoes, changed into clean clothes and returned to normal, except perhaps for a sunburned neck and nose. Now he was in his element, ready for international air travel. I hoped he would not forget the trip we had experienced together. I knew I wouldn't. In Richard I saw myself as I had been when I first arrived in Thailand. I was adapting to a new environment.

His suitcase looked properly elegant as it was wheeled out to the waiting Thai Airlines plane. Together with the luggage of other travelers it looked as if it belonged. Suddenly, it occurred to me; he had never opened that suitcase once on the entire trip to Wang Din Village.

HELICOPTER TRIPS

I had walked to the Karen village of Chawti several times. It was a long trek and uphill all the way. Once I arrived it all seemed worthwhile because the villagers were hard working and open to suggestions. They had a flock of sheep, dug fish ponds, planted gardens and fruit trees, and diverted a stream to bring in irrigation water. They had learned how to use the wool from their sheep to make blankets, and were a joy to work with. I wanted to visit them more often, but the long drive to Maehongsorn Province and the tiring walk up the mountain to their village cooled my enthusiasm.

Sometimes when walking to Chawti, or other hill villages, I would see a Thai Air Force helicopter flying overhead. "Maybe that's the Flying Doctors," I thought to myself.

Her Majesty, The Princess Mother, (Mother of the King) was very active in organizing development and medical work among the Hill Tribes and rural Thai. She organized a group called The Flying Doctors, who were doctors in government hospitals willing to donate their Sunday holidays to provide medical assistance in remote villages. Transportation was provided by Thai Air Force helicopters, whose pilots also donated their time. Eventually, the program expanded to include agricultural specialists from universities and experiment stations. The helicopters made me a bit envious. That would be the way to go. I never dreamed such a wish would ever become true.

I had some contacts at Chiang Mai University and at an Agricultural Experiment Station, so I dropped a few hints about my wish to be included on some of those helicopter trips. Sometimes it worked, and I was notified of a helicopter going to a village where I had work, and was able to get a fast ride instead of a slow trek up into the mountains. Usually, there was no room for me because some of the Thai men took their girlfriends along for a scenic jaunt! Finally, however, I was included on a few trips to Chawti and a nearby Lawa village.

On one trip the village women told me they wanted Dee to come and teach them how to knit socks and caps from their wool. *"Thra,"* they said, "why don't you bring your wife? She can help us learn how to knit."

"Oh," I replied, "The trail to your village is too difficult. I don't think she could walk all the way."

"Bring her on the helicopter."

"Maybe she'll do that sometime. I'll try to arrange it."

When I returned home I told Dee what the ladies at Chawti had requested. "I'd love to go," she replied, "and I will also take one of those new type spinning wheels we received from New Zealand." Dee had been teaching women in sheep raising villages how to card and spin their wool, so she was already prepared.

About two months later I heard from the director of a Thai Government Agricultural Experiment Station that a helicopter was going to Chawti, and there might be places for two people. The helicopter only stayed in a village about two hours; not long enough to do much teaching, so Dee would have to stay there a few days. I would return to Chiang Mai by air, and come back in my Land Rover three days later to meet Dee at the base of the mountain when she walked out. Some one from the village would accompany her.

Dee took her sleeping bag, small suitcase, spinning wheel and a number of knitting needles. The flight took about one hour, and was noisy and breezy, as it always was. Some windows were open, and the noise from the engine and rotors made it difficult to talk to anyone during the flight. All we could do was look down at the steep hills, mostly covered with forest, except for the slash-burn fields located around a ridge top village. We landed on a high point near the village school. The ladies were glad to see Dee and escorted her to the house where she would stay. I have never seen such a hilly village as Chawti. Walking from one house to another meant either climbing up a steep hill, or going down a steep hill.

I returned home via the helicopter, but drove to Maehorngsorn Province three days later and parked my Land Rover at the end of the road, where the foot trail begins to Chawti. It was in a forested area close to a stream, completely silent, except for the sound of running water and chirping birds. I could not see any distance up the trail. I waited several hours, and got a bit worried. Was she coming? Had something happened to her? Finally, Dee came limping down the trail accompanied by a villager, who was carrying her bags.

"Oh my," she sighed, "That was a long walk, even if it was downhill. I wore new tennis shoes, and they are too short. I have blisters on my toes."

Dee crossing a stream on a log bridge.

I helped her up into the Land Rover and took off her shoes and socks, which were full of sand from wading across steams. She did have blisters, and later lost some toe nails from wearing shoes that were too short.

"Anyway," she said, "I'm glad I went. The village women were very nice and even came to get me with flashlights and burning torches when I went to another house at night over those hills."

"Did they learn how to knit?" I asked.

"Oh yes, now several people can make caps with their wool, and can even turn the heel when knitting socks. They are really clever, and so eager to learn."

"Sounds like you did a good job. What about the new spinning wheel?"

"They loved it, and it really is much faster than their old wheels. I left it there for them."

That's how Dee got to Chawti. She did have a good trip, and regaled me for days with her experiences. Too bad about the shoes.

Dee boarding the helicopter to go to Chawti Village

ALWAYS KEEP A COOL HEART

When driving through the hills of northern Thailand delays are to be expected due to mechanical problems or impassable roads. There were always the occasional flat tires, broken fan belt or weak battery. Sometimes, however, everything seemed to go wrong, such as during a trip to some Lahu villages in the Fang area.

Since moving from Chiang Rai to the larger city of Chiang Mai, I was working out of the Center For The Uplift Of The Hill Tribes, a training and extension center owned by the Karen Baptist Convention, but occasionally I traveled to Lahu villages as well to help them with their agricultural needs.

Two of those Lahu villages were near Fang and they wanted to plant some rather extensive fruit orchards. They asked me to obtain the trees for them, and, in an overly enthusiastic moment, I volunteered to bring the trees to them. Although I had never visited those villages before, I knew some of the people from each place. One village, where Sala Ai Shen was the headman, wanted three hundred lychee trees. I had delivered one load by Land Rover, but could only take ninety trees. The road to that village was in fair condition except for the last five or six kilometers close to the village. I explained to Sala Ai Shen that if he would improve the road a bit, I would come back in the Isuzu Elf truck owned by our Mission and take the remainder of the trees all at one time. The Elf was a lightweight truck of

Japanese manufacture that could haul a heavier load than a Land Rover, but it is designed for use on improved roads. All I could do was hope that Sala Ai Shen would get his fellow villagers to level off the ruts, dig out the stumps and cut down a few trees.

After waiting a few days I started for Fang early one morning with two hundred and ten lychee trees for Sala Ai Shen's village, plus ten lychee, sixteen longan, ten pomelo and twentyseven mango trees for the village of Huey Luang. I asked a Lahu man in Chiang Mai, Sala Cai Shen, to go with me to the first village so I would have some help in case of trouble. The plan was to deliver the trees to the first village and come right back to Fang. Sala Cai Shen would then return to Chiang Mai by bus and I would meet another Lahu man, Wallace Pawyo, my companion on several previous trips. Together we would go to the second village, Huey Luang, which had ordered fewer trees. Wallace and I planned to spend the night in Huey Luang and then go on to a boat landing on the Mae Kok River and take a boat to another Lahu village named Huey San where there was an agricultural demonstration center. His Majesty the King of Thailand was planning to visit that village the following day and Wallace and I both wanted to be there, so we needed to keep to our schedule.

We drove to the first village rather uneventfully, except for tearing the truck canvass on bamboo. The nights had been very cold and the vegetation had all been frosted. Those hills were only about two thousand feet above sea level, and frost was very unusual. We unloaded the trees and were taken to the headman's house for our noon meal. We had rice with Lahu hot chili sauce, and fermented beans, which the Thai call *tua nao*, which means rotten beans. If you can get them past your nose they are not bad!

My problems started on the return trip from the village. First, I got high-centered twice because the road ruts had been deepened by water running in them during the rainy season. I tried to straddle the ruts, but twice I slipped in and had to jack up the truck and put logs under the wheels. Sala Ai Shen and his men had improved the road a bit, but still not good enough for the Elf. Still, I was able to keep going until I noticed it was getting increasingly difficult to shift gears. Finally, I couldn't shift at all. Fortunately, we were through the worst part of the road, but still had several kilometers to go before reaching Fang. In the bad spots I had the Elf in first gear, but as the road got better I hated to crawl along at a snail's pace. I discovered I could shift gears with the engine turned off, so I would put the truck in gear and then turn the ignition starter. We would lurch along for awhile until the engine started and then take off. The Elf had five gears forward, but I used second gear all the way back to Fang.

I dropped off Sala Cai Shen and picked up Wallace. Wallace said he could borrow a motorcycle from a friend, so we decided he should go to Huey Luang and tell them I would arrive in the morning with the trees. I was quite sure the Elf could be fixed in Fang. After Wallace left, I started looking for a car repair shop and ended up at Nai Tong's Garage. Nai Tong assured me it was just the hydraulic clutch cylinder and would be easy to fix. At 4:30 p.m. he crawled under the Elf. I waited for him because he kept saying, "*Dio set, dio set* (finished in a minute)".

I realized it was going to take more than a minute and I was getting hungry, so I walked down to the market area to find something to eat. I knew that would be no problem. Even the smallest towns in Thailand have a noodle shop or two. Fang is a medium sized district town which serves as a market center for that northern corner of the country. A town of this size would have delicious Chinese or Thai food if I could find the right place. Both of those food traditions have blended well in Thailand. A large number of Chinese immigrants to Thailand over the past 200 years have brought in southern Chinese culinary traditions. Thais are always willing to accept new food traditions, but invariably change them somewhat to be more acceptable to the Thai palate. Thus, Chinese food in Thailand has become spicier

I passed by one food shop advertising *aharn khon muang* (native food). That would be the local curries of the Northern Thai eaten with glutinous rice. Thais love to eat out, and a party was in progress there. A number of men from the government office, still dressed in their khaki civil service uniforms, were sitting around a round table washing down their meal will liberal quantities of rice whiskey. Because such affairs have a tendency to get loud I went further down the street.

I came to a Chinese restaurant that looked inviting. Facing the sidewalk was a glassed in cabinet in which were hanging whole cooked chickens, glazed roast pork, fish and ducks. Behind the case was the kitchen, clearly visible from the wooden tables where the diners sat. The kitchen consisted of a charcoal stove with three burners. The stove had once been white tile, but was now caked with blackened oil and soot. The three burners were all in use. On one, rice was steaming in a multi-layered double boiler. On the other two burners the cook was rapidly stirring meat and vegetables in two large iron woks. Between the kitchen and the tables was a counter on which were basins and pans filled with raw meats and various kinds of vegetables, including broccoli, three or four kinds of Chinese cabbage, kale, tomatoes, and a leafy vegetable called *pak pung*, which is in the morning glory family. There were also fish, squid, mussels and shrimp lying on crushed ice. People in Thailand know how to eat! An image of the dreary chrome and neon fast food restaurants extending out on the highway on either side of American towns flitted through my mind. Being stranded in Fang was not all that bad.

I ordered *pak pung fai daeng* and *kai mamuangheemapun*. The former is the morning glory vegetable fried in oil with crushed garlic, chilies and fermented bean sauce. It is a very common and inexpensive dish, but I love to see it cooked. The kitchen was in full view from my table, so I could see the cook fanning up the charcoal fire to get intense heat under the wok. He threw in the oil and all the other ingredients. The oil caught fire from the intense heat, as it always does, and flames rose nearly to the cobwebby ceiling. The dish was done in about two minutes and was emptied into a serving bowl. My other dish consisted of chicken pieces cooked with cashew nuts and chili peppers. Those two dishes, together with a bowl of rice, were placed on my table in less than ten minutes after ordering. Several other customers were ordering at the same time, but the cook was able to keep up, although he worked alone. The restaurant was obviously a family enterprise. The father was the cook, his wife collected the money and brought in food supplies from a back room when needed, and two daughters and a son were waiting on tables. The shop probably opened at 6:00 a. m. and would close at about 10:00 p.m. The family lived in rooms behind the shop. The Chinese immigrants to Thailand have done well on the basis of hard work, long hours and frugality.

After eating, I ordered a glass of hot tea with milk. I received a glass of strong tea with about an inch of sweetened condensed milk in the bottom. It came with a spoon, so I could stir it up before drinking. Sweetened tea is always served with a glass of plain Chinese tea as a chaser. Teacups are not used in these upcountry restaurants, just plain glass kitchen glasses.

By now it was completely dark and I hurried back to Nai Tong's Garage, walking carefully down the poorly lit streets. Nai Tong's shop was also a family enterprise. The front room of his house opened right onto the street, and tools and auto parts were kept there. Living quarters were in the rear. Cars and trucks to be worked on were simply parked in front of his house on the edge of the road where the work was done. When I arrived Nai Tong was still under the Elf with a bare light bulb for illumination. An extension cord was plugged to a socket in the house. I cleared my throat to let him know I was back. No response. At 8:30 he crawled out from under the Elf, much dirtier and less confident. He admitted he couldn't fix it unless

I bought a new clutch cylinder in an auto parts store. That was fine with me, so we made the rounds of the auto parts stores in Fang on Nai Tong's motorcycle.

When I was a child I dreamed of traveling to distance places, but I never imagined this South Dakota farm boy riding on the back of a motorcycle through the dark streets of a small town in northern Thailand near the Burma border clutching a man named Nai Tong. The shops were still open, but no one had a clutch cylinder for an Isuzu Elf. Nai Tong informed me I had the choice of waiting two days while he ordered the part, or driving back to Chiang Mai as it was.

I still had the trees for Huey Luang and was determined to get them to their destination, so I decided to take them in the morning by a minibus that I knew went to a Thai village near Huey Luang. Afterwards I would attempt to drive back to Chiang Mai.

Late at night I went looking for a hotel, not with the same anticipation as looking for a restaurant. Good eating places can be found in any Thailand town. Good sleeping places in small towns are another matter. I remembered seeing a hotel near the market with a sign on which was printed the longest word I had ever seen: "WESPEAKENGLISHWITHYOU." In the Thai written language words are not separated. One gets used to it in Thai, but it looked rather strange in English. I didn't care if they spoke English with me or not, but I thought it might be the best hotel in town. It probably was, but they were full. I ended up at another one, a two-story wooden building with iron bars on the windows. I didn't know if the iron bars were to keep robbers out or paying guest in! I had driven the Elf down the street by turning off the engine to shift gears, and, with some difficulty, got it into the hotel parking lot.

There was a young man at the desk. He was the only staff on duty.

"Do you have any rooms available?" I asked him.

"Yes, we have rooms. Are you alone?"

"I am alone and staying one night. How much will my room cost?"

"That will be 40 baht ($2.00). You can pay in the morning."

He showed me to my room, but before leaving asked, "Would you like a young lady to come to your room? I can arrange that."

"No thanks," I replied. "I have a headache!"

My room had walls of plain, unfinished wood. A single bare light bulb hung from the ceiling. The only piece of furniture was a bed with a rock-hard mattress. Gecko lizards crawled on the walls and ceiling. Actually, those harmless fellows, about six inches long, are to be found everywhere, including our own house in Chiang Mai. Because they eat mosquitoes and other insects they are considered beneficial. On that cold night, however, they were nearly immobilized. It must have been about 40° F. outside, and since there are no heaters in Thai buildings, it was the same temperature inside.

I really needed a bath, however, so in spite of the temperature, I disrobed and put on a *pakama* (loin cloth) and walked down the hall to the bathroom. The light wasn't working, but the equipment seemed to be a large clay pot filled with ice water and a dipper. Standing on the clammy cement floor and clenching my teeth, I splashed dippers of water on myself, managing not to scream. Fortunately, I had brought my sleeping bag with me, so back in my room I crawled into it and put the hotel blanket on top. After a while my teeth stopped chattering, and I had a reasonably good night's sleep.

In the morning I went down to check on the Elf and discovered a flat tire. Bad luck was still with me. I took off the tire and flagged down a passing *samlaw* to take it to a tire repair shop. The word *samlaw* means three wheels, and refers to the man-pedaled, three-wheeled vehicles (pedicabs) used for transportation in upcountry towns. While the tire was being repaired, I ate breakfast of rice gruel with a salted duck egg. I inquired about the minibus, and discovered it would not depart until much later, and would not return to Fang until late afternoon. I thought it best to hire a whole minibus, which I was able to do for 100 baht ($5.00). The driver consented on the condition we go out, unload the trees, and return immediately, as he had to go on his regular route later that morning. Those small buses, made from a converted pickup truck, seat about ten people, and go everywhere. Ten may be the normal capacity, but no driver will ever pass up a fare. Up to twenty people may be jammed in such a bus and no one ever complains. This, of course, does not count the baskets of chickens, occasional pig, block of ice and a bag of aromatic garlic.

The bus driver and I picked up the patched tire, took it back to the Elf and put it on, transferred the trees to the bus and took off. In about 45 minutes we got to the Thai village near Huey Luang and met Wallace. We unloaded the trees and left them with Wallace to see that the people who had ordered them got their trees and paid for them. The driver was in a rush to get back, so I got back in the bus and we started back to Fang. We hadn't gone far until we came to a bridge we had crossed on the way out. Now it was all torn up by local villagers who had gathered to repair it. It would be impossible to cross until late in the afternoon. The bus driver was not very happy with this situation, but did not get angry. I felt quite impatient. This trip was getting on my nerves.

I'm afraid many Americans would have made quite a fuss. The driver, however, sat down in the shade under a tree and told me to be *jai yen*, cool hearted. I had already learned that to exist in Thailand I had to accept the concept behind those two words, which means to accept all situations with equanimity and never show anger. After all, what could I do but sit down under the tree with the driver and watch the men working on the bridge. While sitting there I saw the helicopters flying overhead taking his Majesty, the King to Huey San Village. I wanted to be there, but it was not to be. *Jai yen, jai yen* I kept repeating to myself.

After an hour or so, Wallace came along on his motorcycle. His task was done and he was returning to Fang. There was still a footbridge left open over the stream on which the motorcycle could cross, so I abandoned the bus, got on the motorcycle behind Wallace and returned to Fang on two wheels.

Wallace took me back to the hotel where I paid 40 Baht for my room. I hadn't paid when I left in the morning because two guys were sleeping on the hotel desk. It was a bit tricky getting out of the hotel parking lot, shifting gears only after turning off the engine, but I made it out to the main road and drove the 180 kilometers back to Chiang Mai in third gear.

During the slow drive back I had plenty of time to reflect on the activities of the past two days. It had been a rather bad trip, but there were compensations. The people in the two Lahu villages were glad to receive their trees. I had met some nice people, like Nai Tong and the minibus driver. I had enjoyed a good meal, and had a series of experiences I would not soon forget. Thailand is really a delightful place, and its people have taught me that when things are not going well I must always have *jai yen*, a cool heart.

A LAHU NEW YEAR

I was driving out of our yard in Chiang Mai one day when I met Mr. Lee at the gate. Mr. Lee was a Lahu elder whom I had met many times in and around his village of Ban Mai in Chiang Rai Province near the Burma border. Lee had helped a group of Lahus organize a village on Doi Tung, a nearby mountain. His son, Aaron, was the headman of that village, which was called Goshen. Mr. Lee had come to invite Dee and me to a traditional Lahu New Year's celebration at Goshen. "Come and eat the New Year with us," he said. "We are going to celebrate the coming of 'The Year of the Tiger' in the old way."

The Western calendar is commonly used throughout Thailand, even among the Hill Tribes, but the old lunar calendar is still used for special ceremonies. The Lahu New Year follows the old lunar calendar and is held the same time as Chinese New Year. Since Dee is of Chinese descent, we always do something special on that day, so agreed to celebrate the occasion in a Lahu village.

It was about a 400 kilometer drive from Chiang Mai to Goshen village, so we left early the following morning in our Land Rover. We stopped at our favorite Chinese noodle shop in Chiang Rai for lunch and ordered *kutio pet* (rice noodle with duck). We often ate in that restaurant when we lived in Chiang Rai, so the man and wife owners knew us well. They asked how we were and inquired about our children. That was the restaurant where Rebecca locked herself in the restroom when she was about four years old and couldn't get out. She yelled so loud everybody could hear her. Fortunately, the walls of the restroom didn't extend to the high ceiling, so one of the waiters was able to climb over the wall, get into the restroom and unlock the door.

Refreshed, we continued on northward and soon could see Doi Tung Mountain ahead of us, which is known locally as The Sleeping Lady. From a distance it does resemble a woman lying on her back. Goshen is located near the summit of that mountain. We soon had to leave the highway and wend our way up the steep grades of the dirt mountain road. About half way up we could look down on the village of Ban Mai lying in a small valley. It is a Yunnanese village and Mr. Lee and his wife live there. Most of those people originally came from Yunnan Province in Southwest China. Many of the houses were constructed with mud walls and an enclosed courtyard, like rural villages in China. From there on the road really got steep and I appreciated the power of the Land Rover when I shifted down to low range 4-wheel drive.

Goshen lies on a spur extending out from the main ridge and the view is spectacular. We could look south and east over several mountain ranges and lowland valleys. Lost in the afternoon haze to the east was the Mae Khong River, forming the border with Laos.

It was a spectacular and beautiful view, but also sobering. Those mountainsides had once been heavily forested, but now the slopes and ridges were bare as far as we could see. The slash-burn cultivation of the Lahu and Akha people, whose villages dotted the ridges, had denuded the mountain. To make their hill fields, the trees had all been cut down and burned. The population was too dense to wait for the usual long fallow periods to allow the vegetation to return. From our vantage point, we could see the bare hills hoed by hand to prepare the fields for the rice and corn planting to begin with the rains in about two months. I hoped to introduce conservation farming methods to this village, but I knew it would not be this day. For about three days the village would celebrate the coming of "The Year of the Tiger."

"Welcome, welcome," said headman Aaron as we pulled up in front of his house. "Please sleep in my house tonight. The main celebration will be tomorrow." We spoke in Thai, but Aaron is also fairly fluent in English. Besides Thai and English he speaks Lahu, Chinese, Burmese, Shan, and Akha. The linguistic ability of some of the mountain Tribespeople really is amazing. Aaron had a large house, which his villagers had helped him build. At his invitation we went inside, and were served hot cups of tea by his wife. As all housewives of the village, she was busy making preparations for the coming celebration. We watched her make the traditional rice cakes, always eaten at New Year time. After steaming glutinous rice in a wooden rice steamer, she was pounding it in a hollowed out log with a large wooden pestle until the rice became a sticky glob. As she pounded, an assistant occasionally would throw in handfuls of sesame seeds. She then formed the sticky substance into cakes by patting them in her hands. Those cakes, about three inches across and an inch thick, are eaten throughout the three-day New Year celebration. They can be eaten as they are, roasted over hot coals, or fried in hot oil. Already, children were running to and fro in the village munching on rice cakes clutched in grubby hands.

Later in the evening Mr. Lee told why Lahus always have rice cakes at the New Year festival. The story comes from their oral tradition.

"Way back at the beginning of time, Creator God called together representatives of all the different tribes to give them his teachings. A man from each tribe took something on which God could write down his teachings. One group took a buffalo skin and another a palm leaf, while the Lahus took a rice cake. After receiving God's word, each group returned to its own village. On the long journey home the Lahu men became very hungry. Having no other food with them, they ate the rice cake with God's writing on it. Ever since then, the Lahus have felt that they have God's word in their stomachs. All of the traditions that have come down to them through the past generations, they believe, were written by God on that original rice cake. Therefore, to this day, the Lahus always have rice cakes at the New Year's season to remember that their traditions were given to them by God."

That night we sat around chatting in Aaron's house. A pressure lantern hanging from a ceiling rafter provided a light. I kept hearing a bubbling noise in a dark corner of the room, so once when I got up to refill my tea cup, I looked to see what was causing the sound. It was an old man contentedly puffing on a water pipe. The Lahu make those pipes from a bamboo section half filled with water. A small tube extends up from the bottom with the top just above the water line. The top of the small tube is the pipe bowl in which tobacco is placed. The smoker deeply inhales with his mouth over the top of the large bamboo tube. The smoke bubbles on through the water and into his lungs. A water cooled pipe!

At the stroke of midnight, as we were rolled up in our sleeping bags on the floor, there was the sound of gunfire outside. The men were ushering in the New Year with plenty of noise. We were told that the young people would race to the nearby stream to draw the "new water" immediately after midnight. A traditional Lahu belief is that at midnight the "old water" ceases to flow, and the "new water" of the New Year fills the stream. The "new water" was kept until morning when the young people poured it, as a blessing, over the hands and feet of the elders in their own houses. After pouring, the young would squat before the elders to receive their blessings.

Goshen is a Christian village, and after we had eaten breakfast in Aaron's house, the church gong sounded calling people to worship. The entire village gathered in the wooden church building for a New Year's Thanksgiving Service. Everyone came dressed in their best and newest clothing. They believe if they enter the New Year with old clothing their poverty will stay with them for the whole year.

After the service, the young people formed a snake line and wound their way around the village carrying the "new water" in bamboo sections and gourds. First, they poured water over the hands of the village elders, and then the guests. We gave a brief blessing to each, wishing a good year, good crops, success in life, and that God would protect them.

Next, a small tree was "planted" in the center of a flat area designated as the dancing circle. The reedy sound of the bamboo and gourd musical pipes could be heard as men emerged from their homes playing the New Year's tunes that called the dancers together. Like Pied Pipers, they converged on the dancing circle with children following behind. The men were wearing neat black jackets with silver buttons and red embroidery trim.

The women were beautiful in their elaborate dresses. Their skirts were of black cloth with bright colored strips stitched to them in zigzag designs. It was their splendid coats, however, that immediately caught the eye. They were made of black homespun cloth with trim of fine patchwork embroidery in red, white, green, blue, and black. Stitched to the shoulders and fronts of the ladies' coats were all the silver buttons and dangles they had managed to collect through the years. Much of the silver would have been handed down from mother to daughter for generations.

The men, following the tune played by the leader, danced their unique circle dance, composed of much deep knee bending, foot stomping, turns, and rhythmical movements of their torsos, while the women, forming an outer circle, joined hands and kept the rhythm of the dance with their feet and hands.

Between dancing and eating, the men and boys could be found playing their energetic game of top spinning. Each one had his own top made from tropical hardwood. Using a string tied to a stick, they wrapped it tightly around the top, and then threw it on the hardened earth. The top hums and dances on the ground until a rival comes along and attempts to knock it out of the circle with his own top. It is a game requiring much skill, and with shouting and laughter they compete to see whose top can spin the longest.

The most moving part of the festival came later in the day when all the guests were called into the headman's house. After we had been seated in a single line, some of the elders came with two low tables heaped high with rice cakes and pieces of cooked pork wrapped in banana leaves. Those were presented to us in much the same way the villagers previously had made presentations to the headman and leading elders. Each of us, upon receiving the gift, gave a word of blessing to the donor. When I gave my usual blessing of good luck for the coming year, I also inwardly resolved that I would do all I could to help those people find a way to farm the barren hillsides in a manner that would restore the soil's lost fertility.

Leaving Goshen that evening we felt that the "Year of the Tiger" had brought a new beginning for us as well as for the people of Goshen. We had learned something about how to be thankful in the face of adversity, and how to preserve the rich heritage of the past, even while being thrust into the harsh realities of the modern world. As had happened so often, the people, whom I came to teach, had taught me.

CONSERVATION FARMING

The Tribal people residing in the hills were dependent on their hill fields for their livelihood. They tried to harvest enough rice for their own use, but usually, there was no surplus to sell. Sometimes, other crops would be grown among the rice, such as vegetables and corn. Some sesame might be planted for a cash crop, and some marigolds for the women to put in their hair, but rice was everything. A failure of the rice crop was a great catastrophe. If they had cattle or buffalo they could sell them to obtain rice. A last resort was to go to the city and beg.

The villagers began to tell me their rice yields were diminishing. Unlike in Western countries, crop yields were not calculated by how much was harvested per given area. Rather, like in the Bible, the harvest was thought of as how many fold of increase. If a family planted one basket of seed and harvested 50 baskets, that was a harvest of 50 fold. Such a harvest was not unusual on good land. However, farmers were telling me it was more common to receive only 10 fold. Obviously, the land was decreasing in fertility.

People remembered the good old days when they could cut down a forest of big trees, burn them in the dry season and plant their rice in the ashes. The yield was good, and there were few weeds because weeds had not grown in the shade of the trees. Those days were gone. Two things were happening that put a squeeze on the hill farmers. One, was population increase, caused by a high birth rate, and immigration of Tribal people from Burma into northern Thailand.

Secondly, there was less land available because the Royal Forestry Department of the Thai government was doing reforestation in the hills and forbidding the cutting and burning of trees in those areas. Also, large areas of hill land where Tribal people lived were declared to be forest preserves or national parks. Usually, people living in forest preserves were not forced to leave, but they could not make new fields.

Traditionally, a hill field was only used one or two years, so the soil was good. When it was abandoned there were still stumps and roots in the soil that sprouted new trees that grew rapidly. An old field soon reverted to forest, and after lying fallow for 7-8 years could be cut, burned and planted to rice again.

With population increase, and decreasing available land, the fallow period had become shorter and shorter, resulting in degraded forests that were not allowed to grow before being cut for fields again. In some cases the land available to hill farmers was only idle one or two years. With the forest gone, a weedy grass (*Imperata cylindrica*) invaded the old fields. Some Akha and Lahu people had resorted to hoeing their fields and using them every year. With no trees or ground cover the erosion of top-soil was tremendous on the steep slopes. The mountain soil is shallow, so soon the good top-soil was gone, resulting in ever decreasing crop yields.

The resulting poverty had great social significance. I witnessed the deterioration of some Akha villages. Formerly, they had been large villages of up to 80 houses, vibrant with the cultural life of the people. As soil fertility declined the villages broke up into small units, and men drifted off to cities to try to find work as day laborers. Opium addiction increased and young women became susceptible to sexual exploitation. Something needed to be done, so I tried to help, in a small way, by introducing soil conservation practices in some villages.

I received a small grant from CUSO (Canadian University Services Organization), which is similar to the American Peace Corp. The grant enabled me to establish demonstrations in three villages; Lahu, Mien and Karen. I received very good cooperation in the Lahu village of Goshen. The village headman allowed me to use his large field on a steep slope. It had been cropped many times and no trees remained. The grant was for three years, and those years were a learning experience for me as I tried to find the right combination of practices that would bring good results and be acceptable to the villagers. An acceptable practice had to provide three things: prevent erosion, add fertility to the soil and suppress weeds.

I proceeded to measure the headman's whole hillside into strips about 25 feet wide running across the slope on the contour. Two American Peace Corp fellows, trained as engineers, helped me with the measurements. Alternate strips were planted to traditional hill rice, and alternate strips to various kinds of ground covering legumes. The legumes covered the soil in their strips preventing erosion and adding nitrogen to the soil. I planted a row of pigeon pea *(Cajanus cajan)* along the border of each strip. Pigeon pea grows about six feet tall and is also a legume. It formed a barrier preventing erosion, and also bore edible peas.

I experimented with many kinds of viny legumes, some ordered from Australia, but found a local bean, grown by some farmers in northern Thailand, to be the most effective. In Thai it was called *tua nang daeng (Vigna umbelatta)*. It made a dense covering over the soil preventing erosion, and even suppressed weeds. The bean it produced could also be eaten or sold.

After one year the strips were rotated; rice planted in the old bean strips, and beans in the old rice strips. The beans left a lot of nitrogen in the soil, so the following crop of rice was greatly improved. The idea was to rotate the strips every year. Later, I established demonstration plots of this method in some Karen villages. Those plots were monitored for five years, and the rice yield increased every year.

Villagers were very interested in this new system and came to look at the demonstration plots. However, not very many adopted the complete method. If I had become a hill farmer and lived in one village for 10 years I might have convinced the people in that village. In Goshen village some aspects of the system were maintained, such as planting pigeon peas. At least, it was a step in the right direction. Cultural practices and village traditions sometimes discouraged the adoption of a new method.

In Karen villages I conducted several training courses on conservation farming. There was always great interest, and the men who attended the meeting declared they were going to put this new method into practice. They encountered reality in their home villages. One reality was their wives. It was men who came to the training meetings, but in Karen society the fields belonged to the women. They were handed down from mother to daughter. The women were more conservative and less willing to abandon traditional ways of doing things. Also, Karen communities were more organized in the location of hill fields. One year everybody would make fields in one direction from the village. The next year in another direction. That was good planning, because they could release their cattle and water buffalo in the old fields. With my suggested method there was no moving of a field where conservation farming was practiced. Such a field was used every year, so some years it would be located where the livestock were released. It requires a good fence to keep out water buffalos.

One Karen man, whose name was Saw Ja Hae, attended one of the training sessions and was really enthusiastic. "*Thra,*" he said. This is really a good idea. I'm going to use this method on my hill field." I saw him about a month later.

"Saw Ja Hae," have you planted your field in the new way."

"Oh, my wife didn't want to do it that way," he sheepishly replied, and changed the subject. I should have known. Never underestimate the power of a woman!

My village workers and I learned to encourage the women to come to the training sessions too. Adoption of conservation farming practices improved when they were present and understood the system. Success was spotty, but some progress was made.

Slash-burn farming in Goshen Village results in hillsides devoid of vegetation and subject to erosion.

That same hill in Goshen after being planted in contour strips.

Another way toward conservation farming in the hills was to make smaller and fewer fields, but raise more livestock. Some buffalo, cattle and pigs could be sold each year and the income used to purchase rice. With help from an organization in America, called Heifer Project International, my Karen co-workers and I did that. Over 100 groups were organized to cooperatively raise animals. We never completely solved the problem of poverty among the Tribal people, but we did make a difference.

SHEEP IN THE HILLS

One afternoon my Karen co-worker, Sila, and I threw our sleeping bags into the back of the Isuzu Elf truck and headed west toward Maesariang. Sila had been a school teacher for a few years, but his primary interest was in farming and livestock raising. Our Mission had made it possible for him to study one year at the Asian Rural Institute in Japan. Since moving to Chiang Mai, we worked together on Karen development projects. On that day we were going to move some sheep from one village to another.

Sheep are not common in Thailand. The warm, humid climate is not conducive to sheep raising, and most Thai people are not fond of sheep meat. A few are raised in the lowlands by Pakistani immigrants who sell the meat to fellow Muslims. The wool is not used at all, and there is no market for it. The local breed of sheep is small, not very productive, and with extremely poor quality wool. Dick Mann, a missionary who had preceded me in Chiang Mai, had placed small flocks in some hill Karen villages hoping that the cooler upland climate would be more suitable than the lowlands. Those flocks had increased, and I became interested in the possibility of sheep production in the uplands.

The flock in the village of Chawti, near Maesariang, had done especially well. The villagers were complaining about lack of grazing areas for their expanding flock, and wanted to sell some. That was the situation that brought Sila and me on the road to their village. The cooler nighttime temperatures are better for moving sheep, so we had arranged for the villagers at Chawti to herd twenty sheep down the mountain to the nearest road where we would meet them after dark.

I left the main road north of Maesariang, and we turned off onto a narrow trail that led up into the hills. Our headlights illumined a narrow band of trees and rocks on either side of the truck as we bumped over the seldom traveled road. We passed by an abandoned mining site, forded a stream and stopped.

"I believe this is the place to meet the sheep," said Sila.

"I surely hope so," I said to myself. With the lights off, I couldn't see a thing. Stories of robbers intruded into my mind.

"It's already ten o'clock. They should be here by now," I complained. About that time, a shadowy figure appeared alongside the cab.

"*Thra, ner heh li ah?*" (Teacher, have you arrived?) The familiar Karen words spoken by Thra Sa Pae, the pastor of the church at Chawti Village, relieved my apprehension, and I hastily replied. "*Heh li. Sopo oh ah?*" ("Yes, we're here. Are the sheep here?")

Thra Sa Pae assured me they were there, and said to wait. After a few minutes, he and two other Karens came herding the sheep, which we quickly loaded into the truck. I paid Thra Sa Pae for the sheep, and Sila and I drove back on the same road.

We trucked those sheep to the foot of the mountain below Pa Pae Kee village, nearly 200 kilometers to the east, arriving there at 2:30 A.M. Exhausted, we unrolled our sleeping bags and slept on the ground near the truck. I had parked right in the middle of a patch of blossoming weeds which gave off a most unpleasant odor. We kept the sheep in the truck all night so they wouldn't wander away.

Apparently the stink weeds didn't keep me awake! The next thing I knew the sun was shining, and I heard voices in the Karen language saying, "*Sopo heh li*" (The sheep are here already). Villagers from Pa Pae Kee had arrived to herd their sheep back up to their village. I jumped out of my sleeping bag and pulled on my pants just as four Karens came walking up.

"You're here early," I exclaimed.

"Yes, we want to climb the mountain before the noon heat."

"Well, let's give these sheep some worm medicine before you leave."

"What? You mean sheep have worms just like people do?"

"Oh, yes, and worms make sheep skinny, too."

After telling them about worms and how to care for scratches and dog bites, we unloaded the twenty sheep from the truck one by one giving each a dose of Thaibendazole as a dewormer. The people in that village had never raised sheep before, so I would have to come back again and walk the five hours to their village to give them more thorough instructions on sheep husbandry.

Sila and I climbed back into the cab of the Isuzu and drove back to Chiang Mai. A certain aroma seemed to follow us around. Two days in the same clothing, handling sheep in hot weather, and using our rolled up pants as a pillow at night did have its affects. The stink weeds didn't help any either! We also had a chore ahead of us, cleaning the bed of the truck. In eight hours twenty sheep can make a considerable mess.

Sila and I had managed to establish flocks of sheep in 10 villages. Pa Pae Kee was the last, and we drove home to Chiang Mai, smelly, but feeling a real sense of accomplishment. The sheep were finding a place in the economy of the mountain Karens. Sheep were able to utilize the coarse mountain vegetation and provide meat for the protein deficient villagers, as well as much needed cash income. There was also the wool. There was no market for wool in Thailand, but Dee and I thought the Karens could use it themselves. Karens normally grow cotton and spin and weave their own clothing, so Dee was able to teach them quite easily how to use the wool. Thailand may be in the tropics, but it does get cold in the northern mountains, with an occasional frost.

Sometimes on a cold night a family will sit around a fire all night to keep warm. I had seen badly burned children who fell asleep while squatting in front of a fire and toppled head first into the fire. Wool blankets would meet a real need, and some already had been woven in the sheep villages.

I had been thinking of importing some good Western breed of sheep to cross with the local sheep, but the cost, including air freight, was considerable. I didn't have that kind of a budget. However, I heard of an organization in Australia called "For Those Who Have Less" that helped provide livestock to developing countries. I wrote to them, and they agreed to send me six Polworth rams from a sheep breeder in New South Wales. The Polworth breed originated in Australia from three-fourths Merino and one-fourth Lincoln ancestors. It was supposed to be heat tolerant, and is a large sheep with fine wool.

I found there was considerable red tape involved in importing animals into Thailand. The shipper had to send health certificates with the sheep, and I had to arrange for permission to import the sheep into Thailand from the Livestock Department of the Ministry of Agriculture. I wrote to the shipper explaining all he had to do, and told him to send the sheep so they would arrive in Bangkok at night in order to avoid the daytime heat. I also told him to wait until I had everything cleared with the Thai officials. Everything seemed to be going well, and I was complimenting myself for navigating so well through all the red tape, but problems were looming on the horizon.

One day, even before I had gone to Bangkok to make the final arrangements, I happened to meet a man in Chiang Mai who was in charge of a government livestock project. He had just returned from a meeting with the Director General of the Livestock Department in Bangkok. The D.G. wanted to know, "who in the hell in Chiang Mai was importing six sheep from Australia without his permission?"

"Oh, Oh!" I thought to myself, "I've had it now."

Apparently the shipper had jumped the gun and was sending the sheep without proper clearance. I immediately called our Mission Office in Bangkok, and asked them to call the shipper in Australia to find out what was going on. At that time, telephone calls outside the country could be made only from Bangkok. The following morning our Mission Secretary called back and said, "The sheep are arriving in two days at 11:00 P.M. on Qantas Airline Flight #279." It seemed the shipper had also sent me a letter, but I never received it.

I had to move fast. I turned from the phone and spoke to Dee, "Do you want to go to Bangkok in the Isuzu truck? I'm leaving in about two hours." "O.K. I'll be ready," was the quick reply. I thought she'd go. Dee wouldn't miss the opportunity to go shopping in the big city for anything. Within two hours we were on the road to Bangkok. I hated to go in an empty truck, so threw in five gunny bags of red kidney beans to sell in the city. The Hill People had grown the beans, both to improve their own diets, and to sell.

It was a nine hour drive to Bangkok, passing through the cities of Lampang, Tak, Nakornsawan, and Ayutthaya. Bangkok had been experiencing severe floods in some sections. The usual November high tides coupled with severe rainstorms had flooded many streets. We had been reading about the situation in the newspaper and approached the city with some concern.

We found the streets flooded, but passable. The weather was hot and humid, as it usually is in Bangkok, so we had the cab windows wide open. In one particularly deep stretch of filthy flood water, we were passed by a large bus. A sheet of water sprayed up from the wheels of the bus covering the truck. It seemed to me as if several hundred gallons of water came in the window on Dee's side of the cab. She couldn't find the window knob, and the bus stayed even with us for some time, spraying us with the dirtiest, smelliest water I have ever seen. We were completely drenched, and the cab was flooded. Fortunately, we were only about thirty minutes away from the Christian Guest

House, where we always stayed in Bangkok, and took a shower as soon as we arrived, but the putrid water had already given us an ugly rash.

The following morning I went to the Livestock Department. That area was really flooded. I had to take off my shoes and walk into the building barefooted. I found someone who was in charge of animal imports, and he said, "So you're the one, the D. G. wants to see you right away." Feeling like a little boy with hat in hand, I was led to the large, air conditioned office belonging to the Director General of the Livestock Department. It seemed I had not gone through the proper bureaucratic channels, and the D. G. wanted to let me know of my mistake. He did. I listened. I did manage to explain about the lost letter, and the shipper sending the sheep before I told him. The D. G. cooled off enough to give permission for the shipment. "Since they're on their way already anyway," he said. "Next time you start from my office." I assured him I would, and made my departure. While I was in the building, I also arranged for a government veterinarian to meet the plane and examine the sheep. That had to be done before I could claim them.

Next, I went out to the airport to talk to the Director of Airport Customs. He was alone in his air conditioned office and we had a nice chat. He was interested in my plan to bring in foreign rams to cross with local sheep.

"You have a good life," he told me. "I wish I could get out of this office and raise sheep in the mountains."

"Why don't you do it?"

"Well, I don't think my family would go for that idea."

"Maybe you can raise sheep after you retire?" I told him. I really didn't think he would leave his air conditioned office.

He told me how much the import duty would be, and gave me forms to take around for signatures from various officials in his office building. He even assigned a guide to lead me through the bureaucratic maze. After going to ten desks, I finally came to the official that totaled up the duty charges. It came to six times the amount the Director had told me, and was more than I could possibly pay. I went back to see the Director, and he admitted he had made a mistake. He had told me the amount for one sheep instead of all six. *"Maipenrai"* (never mind), he said, "You just change this letter a little." What he wanted me to "change a little" was the letter from the shipper giving the price of the rams as $125.00 each. He was suggesting I change the letter to read $125.00 for six rams. Convincing myself it was for a good cause, I made the change. Anyway, I reasoned, if anyone tried to track me down, they'd never get through those ten desks! With a triumphant smile, he instructed his bookkeeper to change his figures and charge me the amount for one ram. The bookkeeper seemed to disapprove of this whole arrangement, but kept her silence. Thai bureaucratic red tape is formidable, but if you have someone on your side, it can be cut.

By now it was late afternoon. I went back into the city, stopping at a store that bought the red kidney beans, and then back to the Guest House. Dee wasn't there, but the beds in our room were covered with packages. She must have come back to unload, and went shopping again. I took a little nap to prepare myself for the coming night. When Dee came back we went out to eat at a nearby sukiyaki restaurant. Many Japanese businessmen worked in Bangkok, and numerous excellent Japanese restaurants had opened to cater to their tastes.

Before leaving Chiang Mai, I had requested a Karen helper, Eddie Po, to come down to Bangkok by bus to help load the sheep and return with me in the truck. When we came back from eating, Eddie Po was waiting. Dee decided she would return to Chiang Mai the following day by air conditioned bus. I didn't blame her. The cab of the Isuzu still stunk from the smelly flood water.

At about 9 o'clock, Eddie Po and I went back out to the airport. With the traffic and flooded roads, it took an hour. The veterinarian soon arrived, and we chatted together as we waited for the plane, which turned out to be a combination passenger and cargo plane, so the passengers had to disembark first. Finally the rams, in individual wire pens, were unloaded and wheeled into a freight godown. The rams were big and feisty and butted their heads against the cage wire whenever anyone approached them. The veterinarian made his inspection, from a distance, and gave them a clean bill of health. "OK," he said, "You can take them away as soon as you get permission from the chief veterinarian of this province to move them to another province." My heart sank. It was now midnight on a Friday night. Government offices would be closed until Monday morning. The sheep were panting heavily from the heat already, and I didn't think they could take the daytime temperature in Bangkok.

"I'm sorry." I said, "These sheep have to move tonight. One of them is for His Majesty the King's Hill Tribe Development Project, and His Majesty wouldn't want anything to happen to them." Actually, that was partly true. One of the Karen villages where we had sheep was included in His Majesty's Hill Tribe Project. One of those rams would be sent to that village.

"Well," said the veterinarian, "I don't care, but you might not get through the police check points without the proper papers."

"I'll risk it," I replied.

Eddie Po and I started to load the sheep, and found that all six pens wouldn't fit in the truck. We put three pens in the truck, and took the other three rams out of their pens and tied them behind the cab with the pens. The three empty pens we tied to the top of the truck. Those rams were big and strong, and apparently determined to get back to Australia. The three we took out of their pens struggled and butted, baaed and kicked, and nearly got away from us. There must have been an audience of about twenty people standing around watching the *Farang* struggle with the sheep. They enjoyed the show. We finally got everything under control, and pulled out of the airport about 1:00 A. M. heading north.

Later, I was to hear that another American was trucking a bull up that same road that night. He was pulled over by armed bandits who relieved him of his truck, with the bull in it. Ignorance is bliss. We drove all night, stopping about every 100 kilometers to put water in a leaky radiator. At one place we did see what appeared to be a dead body on the road shoulder. There were some people standing around, so we did not stop.

We were stopped at three police check points. At the first one, an officer approached with his rifle on his shoulder, and wanted to know what was in the truck. Just at that moment one of the rams stuck his head out of the truck, nearly in the officer's face, and said "baa." The bewildered officer just waved us on. At the other points we were asked for our papers, so I produced the bill of lading that the Airline Company sent with the sheep. Those looked quite official, so each time we were waved on.

We arrived in Chiang Mai at 10:00 A. M., and unloaded the sheep at the Center for the Uplift of the Hill Tribes. All the students and staff came to see the strange, woolly animals. They were twice the size of the local Thai sheep, and chased anyone foolish enough to get in their paddock. It occurred to me that our problems with those sheep had really just begun. Sending those six rams to their new homes in the mountains over foot trails was not going to be easy.

Rupert with one of the Polworth rams from Australia.

218

THE FOREIGN ANIMAL

The first of the Australian rams to be sent to a village went to Pa Pae Kee, the village where Sila and I had delivered the 20 sheep about a month previously. I had to go to that village anyway to check on the sheep there and give further instruction to the village on the care of sheep. Each ram came with an ear tag giving its name. We selected Tim for Pa Pae Kee.

Sila and I put Tim into a wire cage and put the cage into my Land Rover. Before we left the Training Center, many of the students came over to send Tim off with presents of green grass, and to tell him good-bye. They knew that Tim and the other rams could help their people in the hills and wanted to wish them well. Those rams would cross with the native ewes in the villages to produce lambs that were larger and had better wool.

We left Chiang Mai about 7:00 A.M. on a clear, sunny morning, and by the time we arrived at the Thai village below Pa Pae Kee it was hot. Karens from Pa Pae Kee met us there to take charge of Tim. I parked the Land Rover in a house yard belonging to a village merchant. Sila and I opened the cage, put a rope around Tim's neck and handed the rope to one of the Karens. Sensing freedom, Tim jumped out of the Land Rover and took off on a run, the Karen being pulled along behind. We were right in the middle of the Thai village, so many people had gathered around to see the sheep. Children screamed every time Tim made a turn in their direction and fled into their houses, only to reappear again and follow along behind, at a safe distance.

"What is the foreign animal?" everyone wanted to know.

"It's a sheep," replied Sila.

"A sheep! But it's so big!"

"Believe me, it's a sheep."

"Is it dangerous? Does it bite?"

"No, it's not dangerous. Keep those dogs away."

In that manner we hurried through the village, making numerous false starts down wrong roads and into house yards. Tim ploughed ahead with the Karen man hanging on to the rope, and with about fifty people following behind laughing and shouting. Things went considerably better after leaving the village behind. The trail skirted along rice paddies for a while and then headed up into the mountains.

Tim felt the effect of the heat, and no longer charged ahead. He was panting heavily and had to stop often to rest. I told the villagers to go slowly with him and Sila and I went on ahead. Sila's wife was from that village, so he knew the way well.

First, the trail went up very steeply and we gained a lot of altitude quickly. I was puffing like Tim. We were going over rock outcroppings and were soon up on a ridge looking down on the Pa Pae River in the gorge below us. Pa Pae is a Karen word. I don't know it's meaning, but Pa Pae Kee means the head of the Pa Pae River. It was easier going after the initial climb. We crossed several streams, using fallen logs as bridges. After about four hours, we came to more paddy fields in a mountain valley. "These fields belong to Pa Pae Kee," Sila said. "We are almost there now." Those words were music to my ears. We were right near the Pa Pae River and the trail even crossed it several times. At that elevation, the river was smaller, but clear and cold, not unlike mountain streams in Montana. It took another hour before we reached the village. We went to the house belonging to Sila's parents-in-law, and I flopped on the floor to catch my breath and rest my tired legs.

Sila had taught school in this village and his wife had been one of his pupils. Like many village schools, children studied irregularly, so she was not many years younger than her husband. Sila explained to me that their marriage had not exactly followed Karen custom. In Karen society a new son-in-law is expected to live with his wife in her parent's home for a few years. Parents of daughters gain sons-in-law to help work in their fields, so daughters are appreciated as much as sons. Sila, however, was already working with me in a salaried position so after his marriage, he took his wife to Chiang Mai. Apparently that arrangement was satisfactory with his in-laws. Karen customs are adapted to village life, and are not always convenient for more modern life styles. I had known some Karen men who were living in Chiang Mai, or teaching school in some village, but when they got married they had to give up their jobs and live with the wife's family, helping farm their fields.

On the other hand, those customs do have value. It gives status to women, which is lacking in some societies. Karen women often marry young and have no experience outside of their village. It would be easy for an uncaring husband to abandon them or refuse to support them properly. Under the watchful eye of the bride's parents in their own village that cannot happen. Also, when the first baby comes along, grandmother is right there to help.

Tim came dragging in well after dark. Poor fellow, it had taken him ten hours to get to the village. All he could do was stand in his pen panting. He even refused to eat. He was a long ways from the green fields of New South Wales.

In the evening, and again the following morning, I met with the families interested in sheep and told them what I had learned about raising sheep in Thailand. The biggest hazard was dogs. Sheep are strange animals to dogs and are often chased and bitten. Those wounds get infected very easily in the tropics, and infested with maggots, causing the death of the sheep. I showed the villagers how to clip off the wool from around a wound, wash it clean, and apply a disinfectant. I had brought some medicine and wool shears to leave with them.

The following morning, before starting back down the mountain, we went for a last look at Tim. He had recovered quite well from his unaccustomed walk and was eating green grass people had brought to him. Tim was to die about a year later, a victim of infection from a scratch. However, he fathered several lambs before his death, and thus contributed to upgrading the sheep in Pa Pae Kee village.

The second ram to be sent to a village was Brock. He went to Ee Ko Kee village a long ways to the west of Chiang Mai in Mae Hongsorn Province. He, too, went by Land Rover as far as the road went. Brock was the wildest of the bunch. When he was let out of his cage, with a rope securely fastened around his neck, he went wild. I've never seen a bronco buck like that. After a few minutes of acrobatic display, he took off up the trail on a dead run. His new owner, a young man from Ee Ko Kee named Gae Pa, just ran along behind. Fortunately, he was going in the right direction. Sila and I came along behind, but we caught up to them at the first river crossing. The water wasn't very deep, but Brock refused to wade through. Gae Pa was standing in mid-stream pulling on the rope as hard as he could, but Brock wouldn't budge. With Sila and me pushing from behind, and Gae Pa pulling on the lead rope, we finally got him across. After a few minutes, the trail crossed the river again and the process was repeated.

"How many times does this trail cross the river?" I asked.

"Oh, about twenty-five times," replied Gae Pa.

"Oh, no! We'll never make it," I groaned.

"This river trail is better than climbing over the mountains."

"Maybe for people, but not for Brock."

Brock on his was to Ee Ko Dee Village

Gae Pa was not exaggerating. There were twenty-five river crossings, and it took all three of us to pull and push Brock across every time. This delayed us considerably, and evening came while we were still far from Ee Ko Kee. It was harvest time, and we came to some Karen people who had been harvesting rice. They were returning to a small field house near the trail where they stayed during the rice growing season.

It was the happy time of the year. Although it is a time of hard work, people laugh and joke as they harvest the rice and thrash it. Some fields, like this one, are distant from the village, so the owner erects a field house to live in temporarily while they are working in the fields. At the time of our visit it was early December. The rice had already been cut with hand sickles and the family, consisting of a middle-aged couple, two sons and three daughters, were busy threshing. Rice bundles were heaped around a threshing floor. The man and his sons would bang a bundle of rice against a bamboo pole, which was suspended horizontally over a large mat, causing the rice seeds to drop off onto the mat. The women winnowed the growing pile of rice with fans in each hand to blow away the chaff.

Gae Pa addressed the man, "Uncle, can we stay with you tonight? We cannot reach Ee Ko Kee today with this animal."

"Yes, stay with us, and eat rice with us, too."

"Thank you, Uncle."

The man was not really Gae Pa's uncle, but it is a polite form of speech for younger people to address their elders as "uncle" or "aunt." We tied Brock to a tree near the field house, and sat down on bundles of rice straw to rest. Although the time was early December, the weather had been warm. That evening, however, the weather changed. Even as we sat resting, we were chilled. Uncle came over with a lighted stick and started a fire for us. He asked Gae Pa, "Will the *Galawa* (Foreigner) stay, too?"

"Yes, Uncle."

"Does he speak our language?"

"Yes, but he speaks with a strange accent."

"Good. I have never talked to a *Galawa* before. Can he eat Karen food?"

"Oh, yes, Uncle. He has lived with Karens for many years."

"Good. Tonight we are eating field rats."

"Field rats," I thought to myself, "Well, I've eaten most everything else, so I might as well try rats too." Near the house I had noticed a pile of snares constructed of a bamboo tube with a string noose just inside one end of the tube. The string is attached to a green piece of bamboo that is bent like a spring. When a rat tugs on a piece of bait, the bamboo spring is released snaring the rat in the noose. Apparently, the contraptions worked. I had seen two of the daughters cleaning about a dozen rats. They didn't bother to skin them, but just singed off the hair in the fire.

As darkness settled, Sila, Gae Pa and I sat around the fire talking about the day's events. Down by a nearby stream frogs were croaking, their voices rising and falling as if on cue. A dove called from the nearby jungle. The aroma of new rice cooking, mingled with wood smoke, came from the cooking fire under the elevated house. The field rats bubbled away in a cooking pot. The family busied themselves around the house, cooking the meal, putting away tools, and filling large carrying baskets with rice to carry to their house in the village the following day.

"*Aw mae, aw mae*" (eat rice, eat rice), called Uncle. Many Karens had started eating off plates with spoons in the modern fashion, but I saw that our meal was being served in the old Karen style. A large carved bowl, like a table, standing about twelve inches off the ground was heaped high with rice. The rats, cut up and prepared in a curry, were dumped into the center of the rice. Following Karen custom, we three guests ate first. Squatting around the low table, we would mix some of the meat and rice together with our fingers and eat directly from the communal table. The new rice was delicious, and even the rat curry tasted good after the long hike.

Uncle spoke from near the cooking fire. "I'm afraid the food is not very good."

"It's delicious, Uncle," we responded in unison.

"Does the curry need more salt?"

"No, it is just right."

"Those rats have gotten fat eating my rice. Now it is our turn to eat them."

"Did you have a good crop, Uncle?" asked Sila.

"Just so so. The rats took some. The birds took some, but we should have enough."

The rice harvest is the most important event of the year. Each family must harvest enough to feed themselves until the next harvest. If the crop is poor, they will have to sell a water buffalo, or borrow money at high interest to buy rice.

After we finished eating and went to the stream to wash our hands and faces, the family replenished the rice and curry on the table and gathered around to eat their meal.

Because the day had started out warm, Sila and I had not brought sweaters with us. It must have been about 40° F. that night. We checked on Brock, and found him munching on rice straw. His wool was still soaked from crossing the river, so we squeezed out as much water as we could. Returning to the fire we found Uncle filling his pipe. "How far is it to the land of the *Galawa*?" he asked . Karens in remote villages think that all foreigners come from the same country and speak the same language.

"I come from a land called America. If you travel by a big ship, it would take you two weeks," I replied.

"Two weeks! What do you eat along the way?"

"Uncle, the ship is so big they prepare food and feed all the passengers."

"Have you ever ridden a flying ship?"

"Yes, many times, Uncle. I can reach my country in only one day and a half by a flying ship."

"Are there farmers like me in your land?"

"Yes, my father was a farmer."

"Is that right? What did you plant?"

"We planted wheat, corn and potatoes."

"No rice?"

"Not where I live, Uncle."

"I couldn't live there then. I don't think I would like wheat or corn."

"We make flour from the wheat and bake bread. The corn we feed to pigs and cattle."

"A Karen must eat rice."

Uncle had many questions as we sat around the fire that night. His world was small, and his experience limited, but he had an inquiring mind and a curiosity about far places.

"Why do your people put up the moving stars?" he asked, referring to satellites. Spending much time outdoors, far from city lights, the stars are familiar to the hill people, and satellites are noticed immediately. I was surprised to learn he knew about satellites and that men had been to the moon.

"They want to know more about our world and the stars, Uncle," I replied.

"Then why don't they come here? You are the first *galawa* I have talked to." I couldn't answer that question.

After talking until well into the night, Sila and I excused ourselves and unrolled our bed rolls in the upper part of the field house. The family was sleeping around the cooking fire under the house. Gae Pa piled up some rice straw and slept outside. My lightweight sleeping bag was inadequate, and I shivered all night. When I awoke in the morning, Sila was gone. I found him outside sitting around a fire in the dim early morning light.

"I got so cold last night I came out and sat by the fire," he said. I joined him and thought of my own boyhood on a South Dakota farm. In the winter I would often wake up in my upstairs bedroom with the temperature near freezing, and run downstairs to dress near the wood burning heating stove.

The women cooked rice again, but there was no meat. We ate it with a paste made from chili peppers and small mashed fish.

"Thank you, Uncle. Thank you, Aunty." We waved good-bye as we left. Brock was feeling chipper that morning. The cool weather was to his liking, even though water was still dripping from his wool. It felt good to start walking again and get circulation moving through our chilled bodies. Uncle's two sons and one daughter left with us, carrying heavy baskets of rice to their granary in the village. All of their rice crop would have to be transported that way.

Gae Pa was quite a joker, and apparently was in a good mood that morning. Maybe it helped not to have any more river crossings. We met an occasional Karen along the trail, and they would ask Gae Pa what kind of an animal he was leading. Usually he gave the correct reply, but if a girl, wearing the white dress of an unmarried maiden, asked the question, he would teasingly reply, "It's a foreign pig." Some would laugh, and with a toss of their head throw back a curt reply. Some would look at Brock with wide-eyed amazement and exclaim, "What strange pigs the foreigners have." Gae Pa would burst out in delighted laughter and hurry on, dodging a thrown stick.

We passed through a sizable Karen village that had a very large number of pigs. They were the small native mountain pigs, and were wandering loose all over the village. We stopped to rest there for a few minutes and tied Brock to a house post. Then occurred one of the strangest sights I had ever seen. Those pigs had never seen a sheep before and were very curious about this fellow member of the animal kingdom. About fifty pigs gathered in a circle all around Brock, solemnly staring at him. Most even sat on their haunches like dogs, quietly and intently looking him over. There was no grunting or squealing, just complete silence. It must have been an unnerving experience for Brock. He began to get restless, so we proceeded on, escorted to the edge of the village by all the pigs.

At mid-morning we reached Ee Ko Kee, and Brock perked up at the sight of the flock of sheep there. We turned him loose, and he went running over to join the members of his new flock. He looked so different, and was so much larger than those sheep, that I don't think they even recognized him as one of their own kind. They turned tail and ran away from him. Poor Brock, he was having a hard time gaining acceptance in this strange land.

Toward evening Gae Pa and some of the children brought up all of the sheep and put them in a pen. Brock was put in with them. We gave worm medicine to the native sheep, and put ear tags in their ears. I gave Gae Pa a notebook, and showed him how to keep a record of all lambs born to the numbered ewes.

After another cold night, Sila and I started back down the trail to the Land Rover. On the way out of the village we saw the flock of sheep grazing along a stream, Brock in their midst. Acceptance at last.

HEIFER PROJECT INTERNATIONAL

Sheep were only useful in a few upland villages where the climate was cooler and someone was willing to care for them. There was a greater need for more traditional animals, such as cattle, pigs, water buffalo, chickens, goats, and even fish raised in ponds. I had been able to help some villages with those animals, but my budget was very limited. I needed financial assistance. Paul Lewis, a missionary working among Akha and Lahu people, mentioned the possibility of financial assistance from an organization called Heifer Project International, commonly known as HPI. I had heard of that organization, so wrote them a letter to their headquarters in Little Rock, Arkansas. I received a positive response, asking me to submit a project for a needy village.

HPI is a non-profit, humanitarian organization dedicated to ending world hunger. It was founded in 1944, and was instrumental in organizing donations of dairy cattle from American farmers to send to war devastated Europe as soon as World War II ended. The organization grew to include help to poor families in many countries around the world. Many other kinds of useful animals, beside cows, were also made available. In later years, most aid from HPI was monetary, because animals could often be purchased locally. Recipients of livestock receive some training in animal husbandry and use of local food sources. They must also agree to a policy of

"Passing On The Gift", which means they will pass on offspring to another needy family, so the original gift keeps growing.

We received a monetary grant in the name of the Lahu Baptist Convention, and a poor Lahu village was selected to be the first recipient in Thailand. Rather than just one family, the entire village was involved. A herd of 15 cows were purchased and one man in the village was selected to be the herdsman. It was a cooperative venture, so as the herd increased all families would benefit when a cow was sold. The animals did increase, and it was a successful project. Most people in Thailand did not drink milk, so these were not dairy cows. They were local cattle of the Zebu breed, which are acclimated to the environment. From that beginning, I continued to assist both Lahu and Karen villagers in writing up project requests to Heifer Project. We received assistance for projects of different kinds, including cattle, water buffalo, pigs, goats, chickens and fish.

I didn't know much about raising fish, so HPI sent Russell Gaulin, a fisheries expert, to work with villagers to teach and demonstrate how to effectively raise fish in ponds. Fish ponds provided a lot of protein from a small area. Mostly, he obtained Tilapia fish fingerlings that were available from a government fish hatchery. Russell was a good choice. He was young and single, spent much time in the villages and got along well with village people. He had previously worked with the Peace Corp in The Congo and Pakistan. He was good with languages, so learned passable Thai, and even some Karen. After three years he returned to the United States with his Karen bride, leaving behind many fish ponds throughout the hills of northern Thailand. He was affectionately known as *Acharn Pla* (Fish Professor).

Russell Gaulin ready to transport fish fingerlings to a village.

Tilapia fish from a village pond.

As the animals increased and spread from village to village there was an increasing need for veterinarian assistance. Many animal diseases were prevalent in Thailand, and sometimes caused significant losses. I was able to help to some extent, but was certainly not a veterinarian, nor was I knowledgeable about many of the animal health problems I was seeing in the villages. HPI said they could help by sending a couple of volunteer veterinarians.

The couple turned out to be Herman and Sylvia Salk. They were both veterinarians and had a practice in Palm Springs, California, where they lived. They had also done volunteer work in Africa, so knew now to live and work in a developing country. Herman was a brother of Jonas Salk, and had worked with him when they developed the Salk polio vaccine. They were both in their sixties, but in good health and eager to help the villagers with their animal health problems. I found a furnished house for them to sublet while the owner was gone for one year, and within a few days we were making village trips. They fit right in; ate whatever we were served in village homes and slept on a mat on the floor. The village people came to love them.

Facing camera L to R, Rupert, Herman Salk,
Sylvia Salk eating in A Karen village.

Dr. Salk examining a village goat.

After making a number of trips and seeing animal health problems, they wrote a veterinary manual for "barefoot vets" in Thailand. That manual was translated into the Thai, Karen, Lahu and Akha languages. Training sessions were conducted to train men and women in basic veterinary knowledge, and trained persons received a copy of the manual to use as a reference book.

Many contagious diseases decimating village livestock were easily controlled by inoculations of the proper vaccines. Herman and I met with the government veterinarian for the northern region of Thailand, who had access to those vaccines. Normally, those were used only by provincial or district veterinarians who seldom reached the Hill Tribe villages. The head veterinarian allowed us to use all the vaccines we wanted, and even gave permission for the villagers, who had received training, to use the vaccines as well.

We set about inoculating large numbers of village cattle, water buffalo, and also some pigs and chickens. That was also a good opportunity to train the "barefoot vets". The cattle and buffalo usually received three shots, so three people had to be equipped with syringes and "shoot" the animals as they were herded into a chute. I was sometimes amazed to see Dee with a large syringe in her hand giving shots to the cattle and buffalo. She was a city girl from Honolulu, but she did all right.

Inoculating cattle. Man in foreground is Khun Niwatchai, a Lahu who is now Director of the Mae Khong River Region for HPI.

One of our more distant trips with the Salks was to a Karen village up the Mae Ngow River in the southern portion of Maehongsorn Province. The purpose was to conduct three days of training in agriculture, animal health care and human nutrition. Along the way we picked up Duane and Marcia Binkley, who were missionaries living in the town of Maesariang. Duane did agricultural development work in Karen communities in that area. The boat landing for the Mae Ngow River was south of Maesariang, and Duane had reserved two boats for our group. However, in Maesariang there were more Karen people who wanted to go on the trip, so we ended up with people enough for three boats, although we only had two. We also had a lot of food supplies, electric generator, movie projector and slide projector. We were loaded.

Boat on the Mae Ngow River

One of the boat men said he would make a trip to the village and come back for a second trip. I was in the first boat that was going to make the quick trip, together with Duane and Marcia Binkley, the Salks, some Karen ladies and most of our supplies and equipment. The Mae Ngow is not a large river, but it does have some swift currents and rapids. I had been to this village before, so knew there were some rapids where the boatmen asked everyone to get out of the boat and walk along the bank. It was easier, and less dangerous, for the boat to go up the rapids without the weight of passengers. When we reached the rapids, I was surprised when the boatman attempted to go on up without asking us to disembark. He wanted to make a hurried trip and return for the second load of passengers.

Unfortunately, we didn't make it. Our boat strained on through most of the rapids, but the engine was not powerful enough to get us through all the way. We stalled and starting floating back down through the rapids, until we came up against a tree growing in the middle of the river. Two of the Karen ladies jumped out of the boat onto the tree and tried to drag Sylvia Salk with them. She didn't drag very well and was still in the boat when it broke loose from the tree. The boat filled with water and sank before reaching the far bank. It was an odd feeling to be sitting in the boat as it filled with water and went under. The water was not deep at that spot, so we all got out and made it to the bank. Duane and I jumped back in the river and followed some of our supplies, including sleeping bags, that were floating downstream. We threw them up on the bank to retrieve later. Heavier items, such as generator and projectors, went under with the boat.

A soaking wet group gathered on the river bank counting our losses. No one drowned, but the two ladies were still clinging to the tree in the river. Most of our food and heavy equipment was under water, as was the boat. Our bags of clothing and sleeping bags were all wet, so we hung them all on trees to dry. About that time, a big elephant came lumbering along following the river bank. He was spooked by all the things hanging in the trees and was not happy. His ears stood out and he was blowing air through his trunk as a warning. We retreated back into the shallow water and gave Mr. Big Guy all the room he wanted. Finally, he walked on down along the river, leaving us quite relieved.

The second boat soon came along. The passengers had wisely walked along the bank until they were above the rapids. They stopped to pluck the two ladies off the tree and came over to the bank where our group had gathered. We all couldn't get in that boat, so some exchanges were made. Some men got out and all the women and the Salks got in to proceed on to the village. That boat still had to return for the other passengers, but the boatman said he would to try to retrieve us as well. They had some rice and barbequed chicken we were going to eat for our evening meal, so they left some with our group marooned on the bank.

Our boatman managed to retrieve the projectors from the sunken boat, but not the generator. Sometime later, the boat that had gone ahead came back down stream for those still waiting at the boat landing, and returned with them. It was approaching evening, so the boatman yelled as he passed. "You'll have to spend the night where you are. I'll return for you in the morning." We had food for an evening meal, our clothe and bedding were dry and the Karen men had a bonfire going. No problem.

We ate our food after dark sitting around the fire, but Duane and I soon laid out our sleeping bags and crawled in. It had been a long day. Duane commented, "You know, a lot of bad things happened today, but at least it didn't rain." I'm sorry he said that, because the words were just out of his mouth when big black storm clouds moved in, lightning flashed and it began to rain. A very hard rain.

Earlier in the day, we had noticed a large tree that had fallen leaving a cavity under the roots. We made a dash for that tree hoping to find shelter. The Karen men were already there, but we crowded in with them. It was not a good shelter, but we sat huddled together while the storm raged around us. I had a flashlight with me, so when the storm began to ease I turned it on. Right above Duane's head on the tree trunk I saw two scorpions. Their sting is extremely painful. I said, "Duane, don't move." Of course, he jumped up and got out from under the tree roots. We looked around and killed four scorpions.

The rain ended as fast as it started, but our sleeping bags were completely soaked. The Karen men, accustomed to living outside, soon had a roaring fire going. They had found some dry wood somewhere. With our bags propped up on sticks we sat around the fire trying to dry them. After two hours they were somewhat dry, so crawled in to sleep for what was left of the night. Before falling asleep, I warned Duane. "Please don't mention rain again!"

It did not rain again that night, and midmorning the next day a boat came back for us. We went ahead with the training seminar in the village, but without power for the projectors. Sylvia Salk began to have back pains while we were still in the village, and they got progressively worse. She probably wrenched her back when the ladies tried to pull her out of the boat onto the tree in the river. She was in great pain during the boat ride back to the landing and drive back to Chiang Mai. She saw an orthopedic surgeon, who prescribed bed rest. After a few days she had a full recovery.

When the Salks left at the end of their volunteer time, a large number of people came to see them off at the Chiang Mai Airport. More than one person had tears in their eyes when they waved goodbye.

The Heifer Project work in the villages was very useful, and helped many people, but sometimes there were unexpected results. I was once with a group in a village that was invited to eat goat meat in one of the homes. At the beginning of the meal our host said, "It's too bad male goats only have two testicles. They're really good." I was honored that day to receive one of the testicles to eat with my rice. He was right; absolutely delicious! On another day I was driving through a village when I saw a lady I recognized. She and her husband had also received some meat goats. I stopped to chat with her.

"How are your goats?," I asked.

"Not so good," she replied with a dour look on her face.

"What's wrong?"

"They've been increasing quite well."

"Well, that's good isn't it?"

"No, not so good."

"Why not?"

"My husband likes to eat the goat meat."

"Well, that's good isn't it."

"No, not so good."

"Why not?"

"It makes him" - she hesitated - "strong." I knew she meant "strong" in a sexual sense.

"Well, that must be good isn't it!"

"No, not so good."

"Why not?"

"He ran away with another woman!"

I had to send in periodic progress reports to Heifer Project, but I never included that conversation.

Goat pen at Tee Mu Lae Village

Rupert Nelson

Karen girl with a cow received by her family from Heifer Project

Rupert with a pig ready to be sent to a Karen village.

240

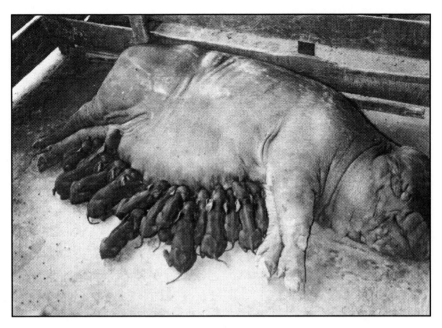

Moi Shan sow (a Chinese breed) and her litter of 22 piglets,
of which 15 survived.

THE FLYING COFFEE TREES

Early on in my work with the mountain people they told me of their need for cash crops. They were beginning to enter the cash economy of the Thai Nation. There was a desire for consumer goods, such as radios, and more of their children were attending school, requiring money for tuition and uniforms. Previously, they had lived in a totally subsistence economy. Food came from their fields and gardens, meat was hunted in the forest and edible plants were gathered. Times were changing. Opium had long been a cash crop for some groups, but it was illegal and the Thai government was increasing penalties for planting and selling that drug. Chili peppers and sesame were also traditional cash crops, but the price offered to hill farmers by local merchants was low and fluctuated widely from year to year.

In the 1970s I, and other development workers, began to hear about the possibility of planting a high quality coffee in the uplands. Most of the coffee used in Thailand was of the Robusta variety grown in southern Thailand. It was not good quality coffee and did not command a high price. However, it was discovered that Arabica coffee could be grown successfully in the uplands of northern Thailand, and could be sold for a good price. I was able to purchase some seedlings from government experiment stations and send them out to Karen and Lahu villages. Within three years villagers started selling their coffee beans to merchants who were eager to obtain this high quality coffee. They were pleased with the price they received and many more villages requested seedlings. They were not establishing large coffee plantations. Rather, individual families would plant 20-50 trees as a source of supplemental income.

However, there were many villages with no road access. Some were a two day walk from the nearest road. It was not practical to carry seedlings to those villages. The only way was to send coffee seeds to those distant places and teach the villagers how to establish coffee nurseries. That turned out to be the best way to establish coffee plantings in remote areas. However, it did take an additional year to grow the seedlings before they could be transplanted.

One year I got impatient and decided to skip the seedling nursery method and deliver seedlings ready for planting directly to the Karen village of Mawta by hiring an airplane. It was a dumb idea, but the more I thought about it the more enthusiastic I became. I had been to the village before. It required a drive to the end of the road, leaving my Land Rover in a village and walking for two exhausting days on a foot trail for about 80 kilometers. One night was spent sleeping along the trail. It was that long walk that made the airplane idea so attractive.

There was sort of a landing strip at Mawta Village. It had been cut out of the surrounding pine forest by the villagers in the hope that Border Police planes would be able to land. Previously, there had been some Air America pilots stationed in Chiang Mai. Air America was funded by the CIA and primarily operated in Laos. However, some pilots were stationed in Chiang Mai and worked as advisors to the Thai Border Police. I thought it best not to be associated with this CIA outfit, but the opportunity of a quick flight to a remote village was tempting. I did accept a ride to Mawta a few years before. The American pilot had gone to pick up a patient and deliver him to a hospital in Chiang Mai. It took 30 minutes. Mentally, I compared that brief, cool flight with the normal two day hike carrying a back pack. There was no comparison. The Border Police used Pilatus Porter short-takeoff and landing planes. Those planes had a very powerful engine and long wings. They had the ability to take off and land on extremely short landing strips.

Short Take Off and Landing Plane arriving at Mawta Village.

The American advisors were gone but some Thai pilots had organized a commercial air company consisting of a few small single engine planes. I went out to the Chiang Mai Airport and spoke with one of those pilots. Yes, it was possible to rent a plane and pilot by the hour. Yes, they would deliver coffee seedlings. No, they would not reduce the price for a good cause. They had one short-takeoff and landing plane, but the rental cost was very high. Too high for my budget. The other single engine planes were much cheaper, but could not land at the short airstrip at Mawta. "Never mind," said the pilot. "We can just fly over the airstrip and you can dump the trees out of the plane." The dumb idea just got dumber. Still, I thought it could be done, so agreed on a day when I and Sila, my Karen co-worker, would come to the airport with the coffee seedlings.

The following week Sila arranged for an announcement to be made over the government radio station that broadcasted in the Tribal languages. The message was for Mawta Village to prepare for the delivery of coffee seedlings that would be dropped on them from the air. On the appointed day we purchased the bare root seedlings, put them in several wet gunny bags and delivered them to the airport. The pilot took one look and said that amount of baggage would require two trips. The cost just doubled. However, it was still cheaper than one trip in the short-takeoff and landing plane, so we agreed.

The pilot took off the doors on one side of the plane so we could load the trees easily and unload them rapidly when we flew over the Mawta landing strip. I told the pilot which village we were going to over fly and he nodded his head. I assumed he knew where to go. The American pilot on my previous trip had looked on a map, took a measurement and flew directly to the village. We loaded half the coffee seedlings, which filled the plane, and took off. When we were airborne the pilot turned around and asked, "Where to"? My heart sank. We were paying by the hour and I did not want to be flying around looking for a village. Mawta was Sila's home village, but neither of us could tell where we were or how to direct the pilot. From the air the ground looks very different than it does when walking on it.

I remembered that the Mae Chaem River begins just north of Mawta and flows by the village and continues on south. I told the pilot to fly west until we came to the river and follow it north. He did so, and we found the village. We could see people standing around the edge of the airstrip waving to us. The pilot made one practice swoop over the strip and told us to get ready to throw out the bags of seedling the next time around. That was a little scary with the doors off, and one side of the plane open. We had to get out of our seats and throw out the bags as rapidly as possible when we were over the strip. The plane dipped and wobbled. No safety belts. I began to realize just how dumb this whole exercise was. Still, it was kind of fun. It took two swoops over the airstrip to throw out all the bags before we could head back to the Chiang Mai airport, pick up the remainder of the seedlings and repeat the performance. It was a hot day in June, but with the plane doors off the wind coming in on us was so strong I was unable to keep my shirt buttoned. When we returned to Chiang Mai the second time I was shivering. I wasn't sure if that was from the cold wind or from fear of going out with the bags. Anyway, the mission was accomplished. The people at Mawta had their coffee seedlings.

A few months later I returned to Mawta on foot. About half of the bare root seedlings had survived the airdrop and being transplanted into the yards and fields of the villagers. I never made airdrops from an airplane again. Taking coffee seeds to distant villages over the foot trails proved to be the best way. Each village would establish a small coffee nursery and keep the seedlings watered during the dry season. When about a year old the seedlings would be transplanted. A little slower, but no more shivers.

THE REVOLUTIONARIES

(names are fictitious)

I hadn't expected the camp to be so large. I had driven our Land Rover past several houses scattered around in the forest when Danny Po directed me to a large wooden house with a leaf thatch roof. "This is Colonel Sa Yo's house," announced Danny Po. "He's the commander of the Seventh Brigade. Stop here a minute while I see if he's home."

Danny Po went up to the house to inquire, leaving Dee and me in the car to reflect on what we had seen so far. I wasn't sure we should be here, and was beginning to wish I hadn't allowed our friend Danny Po to talk us into coming. I had known for some time that Danny Po was associated with the Karen revolutionary movement engaged in a struggle against the Burmese government to establish a free and independent country known as Kawthoolay. Karens are found in both Burma, now called Myanmar, and Thailand, but the largest group is in Burma. Much of the territory occupied by this movement bordered Thailand. For several months Danny Po had wanted me to come to a Kawthoolay camp in this border region, located on the Thai side of the border, to look at possible agricultural sites and give advice on what to plant.

The camp was supposed to be for Karen refugees uprooted by the fighting on the other side. Apparently, it was also the headquarters of a military group. The refugees needed to grow their own food. That was why I had come. Dee had come along to look for an expert weaver to help her teach weaving at the training center in Chiang Mai where she taught sewing, weaving and handicrafts. The military nature of the camp was not what I had expected. I did not want to find us involved in an international incident.

"The Colonel is at the front," said Danny Po, returning to the Land Rover, "but Major Swe Po, the deputy commander, is at headquarters. Just take that road to the left, please." We had already driven about 300 kilometers from Chiang Mai to this place and it was nearly evening; certainly too late to turn back. We drove on through the forest passing an occasional building and many groups of Karen soldiers carrying rifles.

Headquarters was a large wooden building with leaf thatch roof surrounded by a cluster of bamboo buildings which included a dining hall, kitchen, repair shop and more houses. Major Swe Po came out of the headquarters building wearing slacks and sport shirt and smoking a pipe. He shook hands with us and spoke to Danny Po in very rapid Karen, never taking the pipe from his mouth. I only understood about half of what he said, but I gathered that the soldier who was climbing into our Land Rover was to direct us someplace. Danny Po explained that this man would show us to a guest house.

Again we bumped over half-cleared roads and were instructed to stop in front of a wooden house nearly hidden under large trees. There were four bedrooms and a kitchen in the house. Dee and I took one room and Danny Po another. A young man appeared who swept out the house and started to boil water.

Soon we were joined by the Major and another man, who turned out to be a graduate of an Anglican seminary in Rangoon. We sat drinking coffee and talking. The Major was very business like. He got right to the point.

"Tomorrow I have ordered a truck to take us farther on up the road you came on. Then we will get into a boat and travel on the Su Mae Glo River. It would be best if your wife didn't go." All of this was spoken in his staccato speech with his ever present pipe clenched between his teeth.

The Major continued, "I have ordered another truck to take your wife to one of our home industry weaving places. She can find what she wants there and spend the night with a family known to us." He unrolled further plans, "As for us, there are seven sites I want you to look at along the river. We need to grow more food around here." Having said all he needed to say the Major settled back in his chair and concentrated on his pipe.

It was left to the seminarian to carry on the conversation. I discovered he had studied political science at Rangoon University, and had degrees in both Christian Education and Theology from Holy Cross Seminary in Rangoon. He spoke in English.

"About a year ago I came here as a common soldier," he announced proudly.

"Why did you come?" I asked.

"For liberty."

"Didn't you have liberty?"

"No. We Karens were always watched. Anyway, we should have our own country. Then we will be free."

"What does freedom mean?"

"It means determining our own destiny as Karens. We have a history, but only as a nation can we have a future."

"Your life here must be difficult."

"It is! It is! That is the life of a revolutionary, but no matter how long it takes, we must persevere. Now I am a rebel. I can never go home again because it is in Burmese territory."

"What about your family? Will the Burmese bother them?"

"No, they are all right, but a rebel like me would be put in jail or executed."

The Major stood up. "Now we will go to eat," he said. "After eating, our high school is having their closing program. You are invited."

I could see the Major was not too philosophical. He was a man of action. Danny Po explained to me as we walked to the house where we would eat that the Major was not an educated man. He came from a poor village, and had joined the Kawthoolay as a common soldier many years ago. He had moved up in the ranks and was now a major and deputy commander of the Seventh Brigade. More than that, he had been appointed by the Kawthoolay Provisional Government as district officer of that portion of Kawthoolay located across the river from this camp. He was respected as an honest and efficient administrator. He had once been wounded in the leg and couldn't walk long distances, so he didn't go to the front very often.

"Where is the front?" I asked Danny Po.

"Oh, it's over a mountain range beyond the river about a two day walk from here. Do you want to go?"

"No thanks," I replied.

We came to a large house where our dinner was being prepared, and went up the stairs to meet our host. He was an elderly man who had been active in Kawthoolay affairs and now was something like a village headman for the civilians in this camp.

People were constantly coming and going, most of them with weapons. I noticed U.S. made M-16's, Chinese made AK-47's and a Czechoslovakian .22 automatic used for training. While we were waiting for dinner, a white haired lady came over and introduced herself to us in perfect English with a British accent. She said she was from Bassein in the Burma Delta region, and had come here to teach English in the Kawthoolay high School. She must have been between 65 and 70 years of age. Revolutions are not just for the young!

Neither are they just for men. Two women had been busy setting the table and bringing in food while we were waiting. Danny Po introduced us to them, and explained that they were two famous women warriors. One was a captain. They were to return to the front in a few days. They certainly had not forgotten their domestic arts. We were served a delicious dinner of rice and Burmese type curries.

After supper, the teacher suggested we go to the school program. She led the way through the darkness toward the sound of distant singing. The school was a long shed-like building with partial bamboo walls, dirt floor, and thatch roof. Nearby were dormitories for boys and girls made in similar fashion, but raised off the ground. They were very primitive facilities. We were led to some choice seats in the front row just as one class was singing a song in English. The English teacher was asked to present awards to the students in each class with the highest scholastic record. As their names were announced, the students would self-consciously mount the stage to receive their awards. Most were dressed in a motley mixture of Thai and Burmese clothes. Some wore tattered remnants of school uniforms. In the midst of these humble and plain surroundings, the regal white haired old teacher radiated purpose and dedication. She had left the comforts of an old and established family to make her contribution to the future of a nation still in the process of being born.

After the program, we returned to our guest house and prepared for bed. On one of our bedroom walls was a large U.S. Air Force map of Burma and Thailand. On another wall was a neatly printed sign which stated, "WHAT YOU SEE, WHAT YOU HEAR, WHEN YOU LEAVE, LEAVE IT HERE." We slept on thin mattresses on the floor in a mosquito net. With the night insects buzzing in the trees outside the window, I could hardly hear Dee's whisper, "What are we doing here?"

"I thought you were looking for a weaving teacher," I ventured.

"Well, I probably could have found one some other place."

So ended our first day in the camp of militant revolutionaries.

The following morning we were served breakfast of toast and coffee. From then on, things happened just like the Major

said. Two trucks arrived at our door just as we had finished
eating. Dee got in one to be taken to a nearby town where
the weavers were located, and I got in the other, together with
Danny Po, the Major and the Seminarian. We drove on north
of the camp for about one hour, and then turned in toward the
river again. Here a long tailed boat was waiting. We got in and
continued north, downstream, for a short distance and pulled up
on the west bank in Kawthoolay territory to look at a clearing
of about ten acres. The Major explained that this was one of the
sites we would look at along the river.

"Is this a good place to farm?" he asked.

"It looks good to me," I replied. It really did look good. The
soil was a deep, black loam. Limestone cliffs rose from the
upper side, so I knew the soil would not be acid.

"What do you intend to plant here?" I asked.

"Rice the first year," the Major replied. "Our people need
food. More and more civilians are coming into our territory
because we provide law and order, but food is too short. Last
year a child of one of our civilian families starved to death. I
don't want that ever to happen again."

The Major was a determined man. I had no involvement in
his cause, but couldn't help wishing him success.

"What else can we plant here?" he asked.

"Oh, soybeans, peanuts, and sweet potatoes," I suggested.
"You need some variety."

"O.K., we can do that," the Major replied curtly. "Let's go on."

We got back in the boat and now started back upstream.
Again we pulled onto the west bank at what appeared to be a
settlement. Danny Po spoke in Karen saying this was a door
to Kawthoolay. I didn't know what he meant until I saw the
long line of porters carrying merchandise on their backs. He
meant it was a port of entry. One long line of porters, their
backpacks heaped with merchandise, was walking out just
as we arrived. Others were milling around on the riverbank
waiting to receive their packs. Most of those porters would

walk all the way through Kawthoolay territory into Burma where the products would appear on the black market. Danny Po explained that Kawthoolay's main source of income was from the collection of custom duties on merchandise passing through their territory. Many of the porters appeared to be of Indian origin. They carried bolts of cloth, soap powder, spare parts, tires, disassembled bicycles, and just about everything else. It had all been purchased in Thailand and sent by this ant army into consumer goods starved Burma.

In this settlement there were dormitories for the porters and a Kawthoolay customs building. We had our lunch sitting around a table overlooking the river.

"Don't you have any produce to sell?" I asked the Major.

"No, not much", he replied. "We sell some teak logs in Thailand, but get only a fraction of what their worth."

After lunch, we did see one export item crossing into Thailand. Crates containing hundreds of little parrots, once common in Thailand, were going in boats across the river to the Thai side. Perhaps they would be sold in the "Sunday Market" in Bangkok.

We continued on upstream. Unlike most rivers in Thailand, the Su Mae Glo River is crystal clear. We stopped occasionally to look at cleared spots along the bank. The Major was responsible for the agricultural development projects, and it was obvious he knew what he was doing. He had picked the best sites. At one place he pointed out a small stream and said three rhinos lived there. The Asian rhino is nearly extinct, and I was pleased to hear some remained in that place. I suggested they should be protected, and he said that he had ordered that no one should harm them. I had a hunch they would be left alone as long as the Major was around.

At one of the river stops there was a Kawthoolay administration building, bare except for a clock and a calendar. Nearby was an army training camp and a hospital. The hospital was built of bamboo and leaf thatch. No soldiers were in it, but several sick villagers were lying on mats spread on the floor attended by a Karen male medic. Back at the administration building we were served a snack of Indian flat bread and Pepsi Cola with ice. Where in the world the ice came from, I had no idea. It must have been brought in from Thailand. The outside temperature was about 100 degrees F, so I didn't question its source. One of our final stops was a newly planted coffee plantation.

"What do you think of this coffee? Is it properly planted?" asked the major.

"Looks good to me," I replied. It really did look good. A large area had been cleared and planted, the trees were properly spaced, were free of weeds and there was mulch on the soil surface. Again the Major had shown how resourceful he was. To provide some shade for the young plants he had planted pigeon pea (*Cajanus cajan*) among the coffee. Pigeon pea is a perennial shrub that not only provides shade, but also produces an edible pea, and, being a legume, it enriches the soil. I was using it in villages for conservation farming. The Major had figured it out himself. He explained, "We need some cash income. This should help."

The river flowed close to the camp where we were staying, and we arrived there just as it was getting dark. As we were climbing up the bank, we heard elephants trumpeting and men shouting on the other side of the river. Someone dashed by us saying a big old elephant was trying to kill two small elephants. We heard gunfire as the soldiers fired into the air to frighten away the big elephant.

"That damn elephant," said the Major. "Already he's killed two men."

"Why do you keep him?" I asked.

"Elephants are hard to get. Anyway, he belongs to the Central Command, so I can't kill him even if I wanted to."

That night we all ate supper together in the officer's mess across from the headquarters building. After eating, a large group of people gathered in the open area between the buildings to see some 8 mm. movies Danny Po had brought with him. There, sitting in a jungle camp with armed revolutionaries, I watched "Snow White and the Seven Dwarfs", and "Sleeping Beauty". It was unreal. What were a Walt Disney fantasy and an old European folk tale doing in that place? I watched the faces around me laughing at Dopey and frowning at the witch. We could all identify, in one way or another, in the basic struggle between good and evil so clearly defined in the films. I realized the distinctions are not so easily drawn in real life. Do these good, honest people sitting around me have the right to fight and kill to achieve their purpose of a political state? Will they find what they want if they are successful? I really didn't know. They will do what they think they must.

As I was returning to the Guest House to sleep, Danny Po reminded me that the next day was Sunday and asked if I would preach at the morning service in the Christian church. Before dropping off to sleep, I decided I would preach on the Good Samaritan. Surely, that would be more real here than Sleeping Beauty!

The following morning I bowed my head in prayer amidst a congregation of revolutionaries, some of whom had left their weapons at the church door, and then stood up and explained what it meant to be a good neighbor, and how Jesus had told the parable of the Good Samaritan to describe how we should live with our fellow man.

I was not unaware of the contradictions present. To speak of loving one's neighbors in a camp armed with automatic rifles may seem strange. Yet, surely no stranger than telling the same story to a well fed Western congregation in a world of hungry people. In both situations we are faced with the realities of our world and the need for Divine Love to enter into our daily lives.

After the service, I drove on to the nearby town where Dee had stayed with a Karen family. She had a good time visiting some of the local home industries, and made some good contacts with people who could help her in her teaching program at the Center For The Uplift of the Hill Tribes in Chiang Mai. As we drove back to Chiang Mai, we compared notes on our varied experiences and decided it all had been worthwhile, but agreed that once was enough.

CAMBODIAN REFUGEES

There's an old proverb from rural Southeast-Asia; "When elephants fight, the ants get hurt." Throughout history, when kings and princes fight, it's the poor village people who get trampled on. Thailand had been fortunate in avoiding the civil strife that brought great upheaval and misery to neighboring countries, especially Viet Nam and Cambodia. In the 1960s and 70s the war in Viet Nam had spilled over into Cambodia. Eventually, the radical regime of the Khmer Rouge, headed by Phol Pot, came to power in that country. The Khmer Rouge had a policy of forced agrarian reform. They emptied the cities, sending everyone to work in rural areas. People with any education were suspect and killed. The Buddhist clergy were killed. Fear ruled the land.

In 1980 great masses of starving, traumatized Cambodian refugees fled into eastern Thailand. That was when the rest of the world learned of the horrors they had experienced. In May of that year I visited the Mai Rut Refugee Camp in southeastern Thailand, located near the Cambodian border. By that time the United Nations had constructed shelters and basic food was provided. However, there was a need for supplemental food which the refugees could grow in their own gardens. They were eager to do that, so I brought them a large quantity of fast growing vegetable seeds.

Most of the refugees lived as family units in the housing provided, but there was one shelter in which only children lived. In the jargon of U. N. administrators, those children were called "unaccompanied minors". They were orphans. Perhaps some family members would find some of them eventually, but for most, their parents and siblings were dead, either by starvation, or executed by the Khmer Rouge.

Two young American men lived in the camp. They were volunteers sent by some Christian aid group to help the refugees. The children loved them. Whenever the young men walked around the camp they were surrounded by children holding their hands and even hanging on to their pant legs. When they sat down the kids would climb on their laps seeking affection. The young men provided what they could. They hugged the kids, played games, did silly tricks and provided love so desperately needed by the children.

Cambodian Refugee Children

A few days before I arrived they had given the children some paper, brushes and water color paints. Perhaps the reason was for therapy, or maybe just for recreation. The children made good use of those materials, and painted scenes from their life in the camp and of their former homes in Cambodia. Most of the paintings were of fields, mountains and village life; idyllic scenes of peace and quiet. A former life remembered, with no indication of strife and violence. There were two pictures, however, that were different. They were illuminating and very distressing. A boy of about 10 years of age had painted those pictures. The other children took me by my hand and proudly showed off their handiwork, but that boy was silent and watched me. I noticed he had not joined the other kids following the volunteers around. He watched and waited, only his eyes moved.

One of his pictures depicted an execution by beheading, complete with spurting blood. The other picture was of a group of Cambodian men standing in line waiting for their execution. They were guarded by Khmer Rouge soldiers with automatic rifles as they moved, one by one, toward their executioner. The men's faces showed no hope. The execution device was a hoe; the heavy iron hoe used by farmers throughout Southeast Asia. The picture showed the executioner swinging the hoe against the skull of the man at the front of the line. Blood spurted out of the man's head. A pile of dead bodies were scattered about on the ground.

The boy had surely witnessed those events, perhaps several times. It was, after all, a very common event in Cambodia during the reign of the Khmer Rouge. Using a hoe as a club saved bullets. Perhaps the boy's own father, or other men he knew, were in that line. I wondered how often that scene appeared in his mind. Did he dream about it? Many children imagine monsters under their beds. That child knew the monsters were real. Perhaps he had joined them. Some children had survived by being "spotters" for the Khmer Rouge. They picked out adults who acted suspiciously and reported them to the authorities.

He was watching me as I looked at his artwork, perhaps looking for a reaction. What can you say to a ten year old boy who has witnessed such horrors? There was nothing I could say. He resisted affection. He only watched. That boy was one of the ants who get hurt when superpowers engage in proxy wars. I was in the camp for two days and returned to my own home. The boy was left with his demons. I was left with questions. What happens to children exposed to such terrors? How will his experiences affect his own adult life? Will he repeat what he has seen? In my mind's eye I still see him, watching. On that day my contribution of vegetable seeds seemed very inadequate. It was all I had.

Picture of a beheading drawn by a refugee child.
Note: another child drew Moses receiving the Ten Commandments.

A Khmer Rouge execution as drawn by a refugee child.
Note: picture of Lord Buddha drawn by another child.

261

ELEPHANT EXPERIENCES

One of the greater creatures that God created is the elephant. They are awesome to look at, sure-footed, intelligent and very strong. Elephants loom large in old Thai stories and traditions. They are associated with the Kingdom and with kings. By tradition, all white elephants born in Thailand are given to His Majesty The King. Those elephants are not really white, but have some unusual markings. An expert must examine an elephant to determine if it is really a white one. It is not a sacrifice for the owner, as it is considered a great honor to be able to give such a gift to His Majesty.

Most elephants in Thailand are located in the north and northeast parts of the country. Among the Hill Tribes, only the Karen have elephants. I have listened to old Karen men tell of their experiences of capturing wild elephants. Exciting stories of building a strong corral and using domesticated elephants to drive a herd into the corral. Domestic elephants were also used to tame and train their wild cousins. It was a long process and took place in isolated areas so village people would not get injured.

In times gone by, wealth and prestige among the Karen people was often determined by ownership of elephants and bronze drums. The bronze drums, handed down many generations, were used in ceremonial occasions. The elephants were of more practical use. Their owners could hire them out to work in logging operations in the forests. The elephants not only pulled the logs to a central location, but two elephants working as a team would pile the logs in neat piles near a road or river, so they could be transported to lumber mills.

One of my coffee tree nurseries was destroyed by wild elephants. That happened at the Karen village of Teemulae, which was a two day walk from the end of the road. They wanted to plant coffee around their village, and I was through with dropping seedlings out of airplanes! I sent them some seeds and they made a simple structure of bamboo to serve as a plant nursery. There were still a few wild elephants in that area and one night they wiped out the nursery. Really wiped it out. They tore down the structure and scattered all the seedlings that were growing in plastic bags. Coffee was not in their long-range plans!

Some of my Karen co-workers and I once traveled to a village on elephant back. I went with Suwan, Deewa and Cheroen, comrades on many treks, to the Karen village of Pawnawta located southwest of Chiang Mai near Mae Sot. It was the rainy season and they knew the foot trail to the village would be bad, so had arranged for two elephants from the village to meet us.

We drove to a Karen village in the lowlands where the elephants and their attendants (mahouts) were waiting. I could never describe those great creatures as beautiful. They were a dusty drab gray in color with sparse brownish bristles and wrinkled skin, but they were certainly impressive. They were nearly as tall as a village house. Their expressive brown eyes seemed too small for their body size. We boarded the elephants directly from the elevated porch of a house. The mahouts decided to walk. I wondered if they knew something we didn't! Cheroen and I got on one elephant, and Suwan and Deewa on the other. Cheroen drove, or whatever you call guiding an elephant.

On the trail to Pawnawta; L. Cheroen and Rupert, R. Suwan and Deewa.

"Cheroen, do you know what you're doing," I asked him.

"When I was young I worked as a mahout for a timber company for two years," he replied. "I worked with elephants every day."

"How do you tell the elephant what to do," I asked.

"Watch me."

He sat right up on the elephant's head and by kicking the animal behind its ears told it when to go and in what direction to turn. He really knew how. Suwan and Deewa on the other elephant knew nothing about driving elephants. Fortunately, the village we were going to visit was the elephant's home, so they followed the correct trail.

I sat in the howdah (seat) that was strapped to the elephant's back. Beneath the howdah were many layers of soft bark to protect the elephant's hide. We took off with a lurch and the mahout yelled after us, "You can speak to that elephant in Karen or Central Thai, but not in Northern Thai." Apparently, three languages were too much, even for elephants.

We forded a river, skirted some rice paddies and soon headed up into the hills. It was nearly a three hour trip to the village. The trail was steep and very slippery from recent heavy rains. Elephants are fearful of falling, so they walked very carefully. That was fine with me! At times the trail was narrow, with a sheer drop-off on one side.

Crossing a river on the way to Pawnawta

Cheroen and Rupert ascending the mountain by elephant back.

Villagers were harvesting the large bamboo shoots that grew in that area. They transported them to the road on heavy sleds pulled by a single elephant. One sled could hold 2.5 tons of bamboo shoots. Those had made the trail even more slippery than usual.

The howdah was not very comfortable. Neither it, or I, had any padding where it counted! Also, the elephants got warm going up the mountain, so whenever they came to a puddle of dirty water in the trail they would suck up a trunkful and spray themselves. Never mind their passengers! We got sprayed with muddy water several times. When we were still some distance from our destination Suwan and Deewa's elephant started to run and they didn't know how to stop it. It must have been eager to return home. Our elephant, not wanting to be left behind, also broke into a lumbering run that was surprisingly fast. It was like being on a runaway ship with no controls. All we could do was hang on. We arrived at the village about 5:00 p.m., time for a needed bath before eating with a village family.

In the evening we sat with some of the villagers discussing conservation farming on their hill fields. That village, like most Karen villages, was very conscious of the need for conservation. They agree to limit the size of their fields, so there will always be an adequate fallow period for old fields to regain their fertility. They were beginning to follow modern practices of contour planting that my Karen co-workers and I had taught them, using legume green manure plants to restore fertility.

The following morning we checked some of their fields where the villagers were following soil conservation practices. The fields looked good. We left at midday to return by elephant to the village where I had left my Land Rover. On the return trip, Cheroen talked about the relationship between animals and humans. He was impressed by how helpful animals can be to people.

"God has provided for our every need," he said. "Even these large elephants can be tamed and trained to help us."

He went on to tell about his experience of working as a mahout for the timber company. "I used to carry a club when I was on my elephant and beat the elephant if it did not follow my command. Once I dropped my club and the elephant picked it up with her trunk and returned it to me. I never used that club again."

I knew how he felt. When I was a boy growing up on a South Dakota farm we farmed with horses. Heavy work on hot days was hard on horses. My father would let them rest when they were tired. He never used a whip or club on them. He taught me to care for animals.

I was impressed by the forests around the village. The mountains were covered with dense forests, now very lush and green in the rainy season. I remember two dominant colors from that day; the chocolate of the monsoon swollen river and the enveloping green of the forest. Maybe that's why Karen men and married women wear red and the maidens wear white, so they don't get lost in the greenness. Even though Karens had lived in that place for many years they had not damaged their environment. My hope that day was that those people and their faithful great creatures would continue to live in peace and harmony for many years to come.

SEWING AND HANDICRAFTS
HELP THE EXPLOITED

Dee told me about the two sisters she was teaching at the New Life Center. They had escaped a Bangkok brothel by jumping out a second storey window from the house in which they had been confined. They made good their escape, but one sister injured her leg when she hit the ground and never fully recovered from that injury. They were Akha girls from the north. Unable to speak Thai, they were helpless in Bangkok, but with assistance from Thai Government Social Services they had been sent to the New Life Center in Chiang Mai, which that government agency knew was a safe place for young women who spoke only Tribal languages.

The New Life Center had been established by the American Baptist Mission, with Lauran Bethell as its first director. Three houses were rented in Chiang Mai and one was later built in Chiang Rai Province to be used as residences. The primary purpose was to locate young women from villages where there had been a history of exploitation before they were actually forced into prostitution. However, about 25% of the residents included girls who had been in prostitution and escaped. Word of this "safe place" spread throughout the hills, and there were always more applicants than space available.

Prostitution had long been practiced in Thailand, but it was rather low key. Women didn't walk the streets looking for clients, but were available in certain houses, massage parlors and on call at some hotels. However, the sex industry began to grow and became more noticeable in the 1960's and 70's during the war in Viet Nam when many American military personnel were based in Thailand, or going there for rest leaves. The "industry" became a source of great wealth for the people running it, and a steady source of income for some police officers paid to protect the brothels. The Thai government was slow to provide protection to vulnerable women, and influential people were involved. The young women, of course, had no influence. Because of the easy availability of sex, Thailand became a center for the international sex trade. Organized sex tours from Europe, the United States and Japan became big business.

More and more young women were required for the trade, so procurers brought in large numbers from Burma, Laos, Cambodia, and even China. Tribal girls from Northern Thailand were also "discovered." They often spoke no Thai, were unsophisticated, and had no connections in the cities, which made them easy targets for exploitation. They were offered jobs, such as working in restaurants, but in reality were confined to brothels and threatened with severe punishment if they tried to escape.

That was the situation that brought Dee into the work of the New Life Center. Most of the girls had little or no education and they were too old to start attending elementary school. One of the requirements for living at the Center was to attend government night schools and study to achieve their grade equivalents, which they could do from first grade through secondary school. The young women were eager to obtain an education, which they knew could lead to a more secure life. During the daytime the residents did their homework and worked on handicrafts, which they could use themselves, or sell for their personal income. Dee was asked to teach sewing and handicrafts at some of the houses in Chiang Mai.

She was well prepared for that task. Her Home Economics studies, and teaching experience in that field, were very useful to her work. We often traveled to villages together. When I introduced new crops or animals she was able to advise on their use as food. She also learned how to weave with a backstrap loom, as village women did. Tribal women wove and decorated their own clothing, as well as for members of their families. Their handwork was exquisite; really works of art. Beginning in Chiang Rai, and later in Chiang Mai, Dee helped establish markets for those handicrafts, resulting in considerable income for many families. Much of that income was used to send their children to school.

Two Karen women at a training seminar learning how to make and use natural dyes to color hand woven fabric.

Dee also learned how to wash and card wool, so she could teach those skills to villagers who were raising sheep. I had to import wool shears and carders from the United States, as those tools were not available in Thailand. The village people used traditional spinning wheels, normally used for cotton, to spin wool, but Western type wheels were more efficient and worked better for wool. The New Zealand Embassy in Bangkok donated two spinning wheels, and I had a local carpenter make copies.

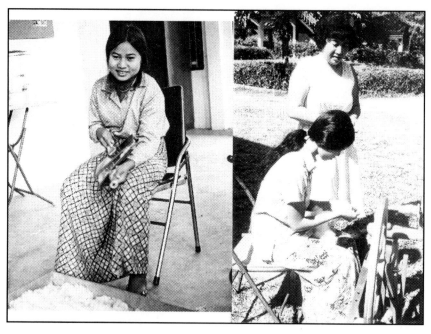

Karen woman learning
how to card wool.

Dee teaching how
to spin wool.

Dee also taught sewing and nutrition at the Karen Training Center in Chiang Mai, which was known as the Center For The Uplift Of The Hill Tribes (CUHT). She taught the young women students, and some young men, how to sew with a treadle sewing machine.

Dee teaching sewing to a Karen student.

Dee teaching Karen women how to weave on a large upright loom.

All of that past experience was put to good use as she began to teach her skills to the girls at the New Life Center. The problem became more acute with the growth of drug addiction and poverty in villages. Some parents were willing to "sell" their daughters, even if they knew the real purpose. Village headmen were often involved, and procurers would give the headman of a village a bonus for each girl he was able to convince to go with the procurer.

The growth of AIDS in Thailand made this exploitation more serious. There was a perception that young Tribal women were less likely to carry the AIDS virus, so they were in great demand to stock the brothels of Thailand. Young women wanted to escape the poverty of their villages, so they were at risk when they accepted employment from strangers. Many were tricked or sold into prostitution and became infected with a variety of sexually transmitted diseases, including AIDS.

Some of the girls already knew how to sew, but others had never held a needle. Their hands were calloused from work on their family's hill fields. Referring to her Home Economics teaching, Dee first taught basic sewing methods and then had each girl draft patterns to make a skirt and blouse for themselves, which they could wear to their night school. She also taught various kinds of handicrafts which the girls could sell. One handicraft that found a ready market was cloth dolls dressed in the distinctive dress of each tribal group.

Three of the Tribal dolls made by residents of the New Life Center.

The girls also enjoyed making quilts, and learned how to do exquisite needle work.

New Life Center girls quilting.

Usually, the girls kept their personal stories of heartbreak, abuse and parental betrayal to themselves, but as they gained confidence in their ability to control their own lives some would confide in Dee their sense of a lost childhood and of their hopes for the future. Many were concerned for their younger sisters back in their home villages, and helped them to also escape a cycle of poverty and exploitation.

Dee with two of the young women from the New Life Center.

The sisters Dee told me about were only two of thousands caught up in a life they had no control over. They were fortunate to find a "new life", but not all endings are happy. One of those girls died from complications of a disease called lupus about a year after entering the New Life Center. Before she died she had found a community that loved and cared for her.

SUPORN'S BABY

Dee and I attended the funeral for Suporn's baby. It was an impromptu service held on a veranda of the Government Hospital in Chiang Mai next to the morgue. A Thai language sign on the morgue door stated: "ALL UNCLAIMED BODIES WILL BE CREMATED AFTER THREE DAYS." The baby's body was sealed in a red plastic bag, and placed on a stainless steel hospital gurney used to move dead bodies. A few metal folding chairs had been placed on the small veranda, facing the gurney. Dee and I had brought some flowers and placed them on the gurney. There were two other bouquets, one arranged by Suporn. Still, it was a stark scene. The setting was not ideal. Some workmen were breaking up a concrete floor nearby, and the noise made it difficult to hear Thra Lodee, the pastor of the Karen Church, who led the service. He read some scripture, said a few words and asked God to receive this innocent soul.

Some patients wandering around stopped to gaze curiously. The noise of the concrete workers continued. The small plastic bag held our attention. That was all that remained of Suporn's dreams. She was 20 years old. Husband dead. Baby dead. She knew it would be her turn next.

Suporn's parents and family members were not present. There was no time to contact them in their remote mountain village. They knew their daughter's husband had died of AIDS and they knew the baby was ill. They must have known that

Suporn was HIV positive. She told a friend, who passed that sad news on to Dee and me. Thai doctors don't like to give their patients such devastating news, so they told Suporn she had a blood disease. She knew what they meant.

I knew Suporn's family. Her parents were kind people. I had sometimes stayed in their house when I was visiting their village. I helped her father receive a small grant, so he could dig a fish pond and stock it with Tilapia fish. Several months after their pond was stocked I was back in their village, and they invited me to eat with them. We ate fish with our rice. "Before, I was ashamed to have you eat with me because we had only rice and chili paste," he told me, "But now my family has fish to eat, and we can invite you to eat with us." I told him I would have been glad to eat rice and chilies with them, but was glad he now had fish to feed his family. Suporn, still a child, was one of the family sitting around the table that day

Some years later, in her late teens, Suporn married a young man from her village who had been living in Chiang Mai working as a common laborer. He probably had unprotected sex with a prostitute, and didn't know he was HIV positive when he went home to marry Suporn. He soon became very ill and went to a hospital, where he was told of his condition. The disease developed rapidly and he died. Suporn was advised to have a blood test, and learned she was HIV positive. She was also pregnant, and later gave birth to a son and named him Yoha (John). When Yoha was a few months old she brought him to the hospital for a blood test, and received the news that he, too, was HIV positive.

Yoha remained healthy for months. He was a beautiful baby, but Suporn took him to the hospital in Chiang Mai when he began to show symptoms of the disease. He clung to life for several weeks. The nurses allowed Suporn to stay with him, and care for him until he died. There were many other mothers with their HIV infected babies in the same hospital.

Suporn was grateful for the funeral service that had been arranged by her friends and Thra Lodee. She wanted us to take pictures of all of us gathered around the gurney so she could take them back to her family, and, perhaps for her own memories as well. Yoha, in the sealed plastic bag, was left behind. The hospital would cremate his tiny body. Suporn went home to live with her parents. People in her village knew she was HIV positive. I hoped they would receive this daughter of their village with open arms, but she may have received a cool reception. There are so many misconceptions about this disease. People are fearful. They don't understand. Suporn lived a few more years and died.

LEAVING THAILAND

At the Chiang Mai Train Station the evening of June 12, 1996 a host of friends came to say farewell. Dee and I were retiring and returning to our home in Montana, U.S.A. The Night Express to Bangkok stood waiting for us to begin a journey, or was it to end a journey. It would return us to a country we had left 33 years earlier. That evening we stood on the edge, between an ending and a beginning. Edges are always a little ragged, partings a little sad and new beginnings faced with some trepidation.

Many people came to say goodbye and place flower leis around our necks. We clasped hands, brown and white, easing the sorrow of leaving a land we had come to love. In every face there was a memory. They were comrades of long treks through the mountains, co-workers, neighbors, friends and old students. Some were grown children of earlier friends. The time had gone so fast.

Thirty-three years earlier we had stood on a similar divide as we left Montana and faced an unknown future in a land strange to us. We had made occasional visits to our home country, but Thailand had come to feel more like home. We looked forward to seeing more of our two daughters, who were living their own lives in the United States, but also knew we would miss our friends and familiar places in our adopted country, The Kingdom of Thailand. Thus, we ended a journey carrying with us memories of 33 years, some of which have been recorded in this book.

Leaving Chiang Mai, Thailand June 12, 1996. Man shaking Rupert's hand is Thra Sunny, General Secretary of the Karen Baptist Convention.

LaVergne, TN USA
17 February 2010
173360LV00003B/107/A